BUCKINGHAM PALACE

H. M. THE QUEEN, H. M. QUEEN
ELIZABETH THE QUEEN MOTHER
AND H. R. H. PRINCESS MARGARET
on the balcony at Buckingham
Palace during the VE Day Fiftieth
Anniversary commemorations in
London on 8 May 1995.

BUCKINGHAM PALACE

THE OFFICIAL ILLUSTRATED HISTORY

John Martin Robinson

THE ROYAL COLLECTION

Published 2000 by Royal Collection Enterprises Limited
St James's Palace, London SW1A 1JR

First published as *Royal Palaces. Buckingham Palace. A Short History* 1995
by Michael Joseph Limited in association with Royal Collection Enterprises Limited

http://www.royal.gov.uk

Additional photography: p. 2 © Mike Dunlea/Express Newspapers;
p. 6 © Tim Graham; p. 128 © Photographers International

ISBN 1 902163 18 4

British Library Cataloguing in Publication Data
A catalogue record of this book is available from the British Library

Produced in association with Book Production Consultants plc, Cambridge
Printed and bound in the United Kingdom by Butler and Tanner, Frome
Distributed by Thames and Hudson Limited, London

Cover illustration: Buckingham Palace, the White Drawing Room

Contents

INTRODUCTION

(*Left*) H. M. THE QUEEN reviewing the march past following the Trooping the Colour, the Queen's Birthday Parade.

Buckingham Palace has served the function of principal state residence of the British monarchy since Queen Victoria moved in to the newly reconstructed building within three months of her accession to the throne in 1837. In the history of the English monarchy, which is the longest in Europe after the papacy, this is a comparatively recent date. Buckingham Palace is, in fact, the most recent of the great royal palaces which are a feature of the European capitals.

In the Middle Ages the principal London residence of the Norman and Plantagenet kings, and their successors, was the Palace of Westminster, now rebuilt as the Houses of Parliament. From the reign of Henry VIII to that of William III, when it was largely destroyed by fire, Whitehall was the main royal palace, but only the Banqueting House, designed by Inigo Jones and built for James I, and the Tudor wine cellar survive today. In the eighteenth century St James's Palace, built by Henry VIII on the site of a medieval leper hospital to serve as a hunting lodge, was used by the Hanoverian kings, though it was considered by contemporaries to be an inadequate residence for the 'head of the richest and most powerful kingdom in Europe'. The creation of Buckingham Palace as an appropriate symbol of national greatness in the aftermath of the victories of the Napoleonic Wars was the work of George IV, a great patron of the arts, whose principal monuments are Windsor Castle, Buckingham Palace, Brighton Pavilion and Regent's Park.

BUCKINGHAM HOUSE, THE
ENTRANCE FRONT: Engraving from
Kip & Knyff's *Nouveau Théâtre de la
Grande Bretagne*, 1725. The new house
was built for the Duke of Buckingham
to the design of William Talman,
Comptroller of the Office of Works,
and Captain William Winde. The
plan, with flanking pavilions, was
inspired by the Italian architect
Andrea Palladio and was then a
novelty in England. The forecourt
had a fountain with statues of
Neptune and tritons, and elaborate
iron railings and gates by the
Huguenot smith, Jean Tijou. The
main block is incorporated in the
west wing of the present palace.

Buckingham House in St James Park belonging to the Most Noble & Potent Prin
Gentleman of ye Bed-Chamber to K: Ch. 2d. Colonell of the Holland Regiment and Governour of Hull
k. Iames. 2d Created Marqueß of Normanby by K. Will. & Qu: Mary. and one of their Maties mos.

Iohn Sheffield Baron of Botternick, Earl of Mulgrave, Kn:t of y:e mo:st Noble Order of y:e Garter.
Vice-Admirall of Yorkshire Northumberland & Bishoprick of Durham and Lord Chamberlain to
Hon:ble Privy Councell, & by Qu: Anne Duke of y:e County of Buckingham & of Normanby & Lord PrivySeal.

SITI LÆTANTUR LARES

CHAPTER ONE

THE EARLY HISTORY OF THE PALACE

From Mulberry Garden to Queen's House

ALLAN RAMSAY: *GEORGE III*, 1762. The splendid official portraits of George III and Queen Charlotte in Coronation robes were painted by the Scottish artist Allan Ramsay on the recommendation of the Prime Minister, Lord Bute. Both in the composition and in the painting of the robes Ramsay shows his awareness of contemporary French painting. This has been described as the most distinguished state portrait of a British monarch since the time of Sir Anthony van Dyck.

Though it is today the official London residence of the sovereign as head of state of the United Kingdom, Buckingham Palace still bears the name of the non-royal duke who began the existing building two and a half centuries ago. Part of the Duke of Buckingham's original brick structure also survives, embedded within the present larger, stone-faced quadrangle. The history of Buckingham Palace is that of the successive enlargement and remodelling of an older, smaller house over a period of a century and a half, to create the existing elaborate late neo-classical structure with its imperial façades and richly decorated and furnished state rooms.

The history of the Palace site can be traced back one hundred years earlier than the Duke of Buckingham's house, to the reign of James I, when part of the area at the west of St James's Park was leased to William Stallinge as a mulberry garden to breed silk worms in a short-lived economic experiment. Some years later, in 1633, Lord Goring created on a site next to the mulberry garden a 'fair house and other convenient buildings and outhouses, and upon the other part of it made the fountain garden, a terrace walk, a courtyard and laundry yard.' A drawing on a map of 1675 shows an unremarkable, plain house with four gables, to the south of the existing building.

In 1665 the house was let to 'Mr. Secretary Bennett', later the Earl of Arlington. The diarist John Evelyn described it at that time as 'ill built, but the place capable of being made a pretty villa'.

In September 1675 the old house was burnt down. John Evelyn noted in his diary that Goring House was 'consum'd to the ground, with exceeding loss of hangings, plate, rare pictures and cabinets;

BUCKINGHAM HOUSE, the garden front: detail from an oil painting attributed to Adrian van Diest (*c.* 1700), recently acquired for the Royal Collection. Beyond the trees of St James's Park can be seen Westminster Abbey. The brick wall in the foreground enclosed the elaborate formal garden laid out for the Duke of Buckingham under the direction of Henry Wise, the royal gardener. The lead statues on the roof depicted Apollo, Liberty, Equity, Mercury, Truth and Secrecy.

in a word, nothing almost was saved of the best and most princely furniture that any subject had in England.' Lord Arlington, hitherto only a tenant, purchased the lease of the place in 1677 and rebuilt the house in the same year in a more up-to-date Anglo-Dutch style, with a domed cupola in the middle of the roof, similar to houses such as Belton House in Lincolnshire. The principal internal feature of Arlington House was a long gallery overlooking St James's Park with nine sash windows, marble-topped pier tables and full-length portraits in gilded frames. Evelyn described the new house as 'a very fine, noble place'. Whereas old Goring House had faced south, the new Arlington House looked out eastwards over the park, which had been remodelled by Charles II with formal water and avenues of trees in the French manner.

Lord Arlington lived just long enough to officiate as Lord Chamberlain at the Coronation of James II in 1685. He settled the house at his death on his daughter and her husband, Henry Fitzroy, 1st Duke of Grafton. But at the latter's premature death from a wound received at the Siege of Cork in 1690, the house passed to their son, who was then only seven years old. It was therefore once again let out to tenants. In 1698 it was taken by John Sheffield, Earl of

VIEW FROM OLD BUCKINGHAM HOUSE. The centre of the Duke of Buckingham's house was aligned on the avenue along the north side of St James's Park, with the spires of the City churches and the dome of St Paul's Cathedral in the distance.

Mulgrave and Marquess of Normanby, who was created Duke of Buckingham in 1703. A year earlier he had bought the house outright from the trustees of the young Duke of Grafton. It was mainly a freehold, but a small portion of the site was a Crown lease, and this was to play an important role in the future history of the place.

The Duke of Buckingham immediately set about extravagant improvements. He demolished Arlington House, though it was only thirty years old, and built a grander new house slightly to the north, nearer to Green Park and centred on the Mall, Charles II's avenue along the north side of St James's Park. This building forms the nucleus of the present main block of the Palace and dictates the dimensions of the Grand Entrance Hall and the ground floor.

Work began with the laying-out of a large formal garden with lime avenues, a parterre and a bowling green at the back of the site, under the direction of Henry Wise, the royal gardener. In front of the new house, and encroaching into the park, the Duke laid out a formal forecourt with an iron palisade by Jean Tijou, the renowned Huguenot ironsmith, and a 'great basin with the figures of Neptune and the Triton in a water work'.

The house itself was designed and built with the assistance of two architects. William Talman, Comptroller of the Works to William

BAROGRAPH MADE FOR
GEORGE III, BY ALEXANDER
CUMMING. This was commissioned
by George III in 1765 and cost £1,178.
The case is of kingwood and
mahogany with chased gilt bronze
ornaments of the highest quality.

III, may have drawn up the original plans and Captain William Winde, a retired soldier, 'conducted' the work of construction. John Fitch built the main structure by contract for £7,000. The plan comprised a central block with two flanking pavilions connected by colonnades, following the precedent of Palladio's villas in the Veneto, but then a novelty in England, the only other English precursor being Stoke Park in Northamptonshire. The principal façade was embellished with Corinthian pilasters and an attic storey sporting lead statues of Apollo, Liberty, Equity, Mercury, Truth and Secrecy. The sophisticated design of the new Buckingham House, as it was now called, was very influential and became the source for many English country houses which still exist, such as Wotton House and Chicheley House in Buckinghamshire. The interior had a hall paved with marble, a grand staircase and painted decorations in the rooms by the Continental artists Sebastiano Ricci from Venice and Louis Laguerre from Versailles.

The Duke took great pleasure and pride in his new house, as was expressed in the carved Latin inscription on the entrance front: *'Sic situ Laetantur Lares'* (The Household Gods delight in such a situation). The setting of the new house between St James's Park and Hyde Park, looking down the avenue of limes and elms towards Westminster and the City of London, with the dome of St Paul's visible in the distance, was its most attractive feature. The new Buckingham House was more a country residence on the edge of London than a town house, and to some extent it has retained that character ever since, thanks to its extensive parkland setting.

Buckingham House remained the property of the Dukes of Buckingham until the mid-eighteenth century. A small part of the site was not freehold but a Crown lease (having been enclosed out of St James's Park). A problem over this lease enabled George III to acquire the whole site in 1761 as a private residence, following his marriage to Charlotte of Mecklenburg-Strelitz. His aim was to use the house as a comfortable family home adjacent to St James's Palace where the somewhat antiquated state rooms continued to be used, as they had been since the reign of George I, for court functions. The King wrote to his Prime Minister Lord Bute that the new house was 'not meant for a Palace but a retreat'. George III had studied architecture as part of his general education and on acceding to the throne had created a new post of Architect of Works in 1761, which was shared by the two leaders of the profession, Robert Adam and Sir William Chambers. The latter was given the job of remodelling and modernizing

BUCKINGHAM HOUSE: the
entrance side as remodelled for
George III by Sir William Chambers
with simpler railings and the more
baroque ornaments shaved off. The
octagon behind the left pavilion was
one of the King's libraries.

Buckingham House between 1762 and 1774 at a cost of £73,000.

The exterior was, in the words of the biographer of William
Chambers, John Harris, generally 'scrubbed with a neo-classic
brush', to bring it up to date. The baroque qualities of the original
design were long out of fashion when George III bought the house,
so it was decided to encase it in smooth new brick, omitting the
pilasters from the corners and hiding the basement storey by raising
the forecourt. Tijou's grand iron screens in front were replaced by
simpler railings, symbolizing George III's unpretentious taste.
Additional space was provided in new wings on either side of the
Duke of Buckingham's garden front. The resulting house was a villa
rather than a palace and emphatically a private residence of the
royal family, not the seat of the court, which remained St James's.
This distinction is the origin of the anomaly whereby foreign
ambassadors are still, two centuries later, accredited to the Court
of St James.

The King's rooms on the ground floor at Buckingham House
were fitted up neatly but, by royal standards, extremely plainly.
There were, for instance, no carpets, as the King thought them
unhealthy. John Adams, the American Minister to England who

JAMES STEPHANOFF: *THE OCTAGON LIBRARY*. This was the principal of the four libraries added by George III in the 1760s to house his growing collection of books. The King exercised detailed control over the fitting-up of these rooms. The octagonal central table (later remodelled) and the clock survive in the Royal Library at Windsor Castle. The libraries were the King's private retreat and could only be entered through his bedroom. This is one of a number of watercolours commissioned for W. H. Pyne's *Royal Residences*, published in 1819.

visited Buckingham House in 1783, was struck by the elegance of the interior and in particular by the simplicity of the King's rooms: 'In every apartment of the whole house, the same taste, the same judgement, the same elegance, the same simplicity, without the smallest affectation, ostentation, profusion, or meanness.' They comprised the King's Bedroom, the Dining Room and the 'Warm Room'.

The four grandest rooms, including a two-storeyed octagon in the south wing, were occupied by the Library, which continued to be expanded throughout the reign to keep pace with the King's bibliomania. By the time of his death in 1820 it comprised 67,000 volumes and had cost £120,000. (It is now the King's Library in the British Library.) On George III's accession there had been no royal library, because that formed by his predecessors from Henry VIII onwards, consisting of some 9,000 books, had been given in 1757 to the newly founded British Museum by George II. To replace it, George III immediately began forming a library of his own, replete

JAMES STEPHANOFF: *THE GREAT OR WEST LIBRARY*. Above the chimneypiece is a large map and wind-dial connected to an external weather vane on the roof, which enabled the King to conjecture how his fleet might be faring.

not just with books but also with maps and medals. The bookcases, folio and medal cabinets for all these, as well as finely carved mahogany furniture for the Queen's rooms upstairs, were commissioned from the King's favourite cabinet-makers, William Vile (of Vile & Cobb) and John Bradburn, from 1761 to 1767. Vile supplied cabinets to house 1,600 medals in 1761 and 1762, and a further 1,385 medals in 1766 and 1767, which gives an indication of the scale of the King's collecting in the first ten years of his reign. In 1767 Bradburn made map presses costing £260 10s. and stands and frames for hanging maps.

The King exercised detailed supervision over the finishing of these rooms and the plans of the cabinet-makers were submitted to him for his approval, including Bradburn's specification for fitting up the Upper Library. The King himself sometimes provided rough sketches for the hanging of the pictures and so forth to guide the architects, decorators and cabinet-makers; some of these sketches survive in the Royal Library at Windsor Castle. He was meticulous

JAMES STEPHANOFF: *THE GREAT STAIRCASE AT BUCKINGHAM HOUSE* in 1819. The wall and ceiling paintings by Laguerre survived from the Duke of Buckingham's time. The doorway in the feigned niche on the landing was created by Sir William Chambers in the 1760s, and the imperial-plan stone staircase was inserted by James Wyatt, the royal surveyor-general, in 1799.

about details, and if some feature of a design displeased him he amended it in his own hand.

Queen Charlotte's rooms on the first floor were far more richly furnished than the King's below and were filled with her collections of china, ivories, snuffboxes, étuis, jade, lacquer and pretty objets de vertu. The Queen shared many of her husband's tastes, but was less conservative and less averse to lavish effects. Mrs Lybbe Powys, an inveterate visitor of houses, gained access to Buckingham House in 1767 and found the Queen's rooms much grander and more elaborately furnished than the King's. And she was impressed by the Queen's collection of 'curiosities from every nation...The most capital pictures, the finest Dresden and other china, cabinets of more minute curiosities', mostly sold at Christie's after her death in 1818. The old two-storeyed Saloon of Buckingham House was completely redecorated in a cool grey and gold neo-classical scheme, 'painted in the antique taste' by Giovanni Battista Cipriani (an Italian artist brought to England from Rome by William Chambers), aided by William Oram (of the Office of Works), with pilaster strips and gilt oval looking-glasses. The white marble

JAMES STEPHANOFF: *THE SALOON AT BUCKINGHAM HOUSE.* This two-storeyed room occupied the central three bays of the entrance front of the Duke of Buckingham's house. It was redesigned by Sir William Chambers for George III. The marble chimneypiece surmounted by a clock was designed by Robert Adam and carved by John Bacon; it is now at Windsor Castle. The gilt framed sofas are now in the Picture Gallery at Buckingham Palace.

JOHANN ZOFFANY: *QUEEN CHARLOTTE WITH HER TWO ELDEST SONS, GEORGE, THE PRINCE OF WALES AND FREDERICK, LATER DUKE OF YORK c. 1765.* It has been suggested that this family group is set in the ground-floor rooms on the garden side of Buckingham House, but embellished with some of the richer furnishings from the Queen's rooms on the first floor. This is the only view of the King's rooms with their restrained architecture and plain grey-green paintwork.

chimneypiece, incorporating a clock, was sculpted by John Bacon to Robert Adam's design (it is now at Windsor Castle). The whole ensemble, subdued but undoubtedly regal, served as the Queen's Throne Room when she started holding her 'drawing-rooms' there rather than at St James's, after the establishment of the Regency.

In the centre of the garden front, behind the Saloon, was the Crimson Drawing Room with the Queen's Dressing Room adjoining. Both had elegant stucco ceilings embellished with inset paintings by Cipriani, one designed by Robert Adam and one by

JOHANN ZOFFANY: *GEORGE, PRINCE OF WALES AND FREDERICK, LATER DUKE OF YORK, c. 1765.* The children are depicted in Queen Charlotte's dressing room on the first floor, which Horace Walpole described as 'hung with red damask and pictures'. The marble chimneypiece by Sir William Chambers is now at Windsor Castle, as are the van Dyck portraits of the children of Charles I and the Villiers family.

Sir William Chambers. The room to the north was the Queen's Bedroom and to the south was the Queen's Breakfast Room, on the garden front. A visitor in 1802 commented: 'Here are the comforts of a family home, with the grandeur and some of the ornaments of a palace.' The atmosphere of the house as a family home is captured in Johann Zoffany's attractive portraits of Queen Charlotte and her two elder sons, the Prince of Wales and Frederick, Duke of York. Fourteen of the royal couple's fifteen children were born at Buckingham House.

The rooms, however, did not then make a formal apartment for traditional court functions: these continued to be held at first in the old state rooms at St James's Palace, which were redecorated and much gilded in 1794. The regular functions, until the breakdown of the King's health later in the reign, chiefly comprised levees and drawing-rooms; there were also the occasional court ball and formal receptions of foreign ambassadors. Levees were purely male occasions held by the King, which, until his illness, took place regularly on Wednesdays and Fridays (and until 1788 on Mondays when Parliament was sitting) in the morning. The King received formal addresses in the Presence Chamber, such as that presented by the Duke of Norfolk in 1778 on behalf of the Catholics of Britain and Ireland, which resulted in the first degree of Catholic Emancipation. Audiences to his Ministers were granted by the King in the State Bedroom, while the general circle formed in the Drawing Room, where the King walked round saying a few words to everyone and occasionally snubbing somebody of whose public actions he disapproved.

Attendance at levees was more or less compulsory for anyone prominent in public and official life. Their purpose was partly ceremonial, in that they comprised presentations of individuals to the monarch, but they also still related directly to the business of government, as they were still the occasion when addresses and petitions were presented and offices distributed. They could be exhausting for the King: he might well be on his feet continuously from 11.00 a.m. to 5.00 p.m. without refreshment.

Drawing-rooms were a weekly event on Thursdays and were attended by both sexes. They took place in the morning, first at St James's but later in the reign in the Queen's Rooms at Buckingham House. In the early part of the reign, when the King and Queen were in London, a drawing-room was also held on Sundays after church. But there were fewer drawing-rooms as time passed, and by the last years of George III's reign, when the Prince Regent stood in for his father, they were held only 'two or four times a year, and everybody man or woman that assumes the name of gentleman or lady go to it'. In the last years of his reign, George III spent more time in the country at Windsor Castle and Kew, a smaller country house where his parents had lived, than in London, but Queen Charlotte continued to use Buckingham House regularly till her death in 1818.

As well as being responsible for the purchase of Buckingham

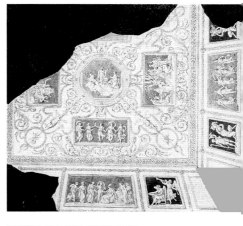

DESIGN FOR THE CEILING OF QUEEN CHARLOTTE'S DRESSING ROOM, LATER THE SECOND DRAWING ROOM, BY CIPRIANI. This ceiling was one of a pair executed by Cipriani, under Robert Adam's and Sir William Chambers' supervision, and described by Horace Walpole as being 'newly painted in the antique taste'. This drawing shows the ceiling in fragmentary state, as if it had been discovered in the excavations of a Roman villa.

JAMES STEPHANOFF: *QUEEN CHARLOTTE'S DRESSING ROOM, LATER THE SECOND DRAWING ROOM AT BUCKINGHAM HOUSE.* The room was designed by Sir William Chambers and the ceiling decorated by Cipriani in the antique Roman manner *en suite* with that in the adjoining Crimson Drawing Room. The crimson damask on the walls of both rooms was supplied by the mercer Robert Carr. The room was sometimes described as the Queen's Warm Room, indicating its function as her private sitting room.

House as a royal residence, George III played an important role in assembling the magnificent collection which is today its principal glory. Most of Charles I's unequalled collection of paintings was dispersed following his execution in 1649, but after the Restoration of the monarchy in 1660 Charles II reassembled what he could. Much of the earlier part of the collection is today hung at Hampton Court or Windsor Castle and the contents of Buckingham Palace, with a few notable exceptions, chiefly reflect Georgian and Victorian taste.

It is often said that George IV was the only true collector and connoisseur of art produced by the Hanoverian dynasty. This view is not borne out by the facts. Although George I was a somewhat philistine figure, more interested in his own principality of Hanover than his English palaces and possessions, George II's wife, Caroline of Ansbach, introduced a more civilized strain into the family, which flourished in succeeding generations: both her son Frederick, Prince of Wales and his son George III were active and discerning patrons. Queen Caroline was a patron of the architect William Kent and sculptor Michael Rysbrack. She had a keen interest in landscape gardening, expressed principally in Kensington Gardens and Hyde Park where the Serpentine, an artificial lake, was created under her aegis in 1730. She also collected books and commissioned a splendid library to house them at St James's Palace. The library was designed by William Kent but, unfortunately, demolished in 1825.

Although her eldest son, Frederick, Prince of Wales, was a

G. HUMPHREY: THE FORECOURT OF BUCKINGHAM HOUSE AND GREEN PARK, 1822: an engraving showing a crowd of guests arriving for a royal drawing-room.

JEAN BAPTISTE VAN LOO:
FREDERICK, PRINCE OF WALES, 1742.
The eldest son of George II and
father of George III was a considerable royal patron but due to his early
death in 1751 his achievements have
been underestimated. He pioneered
the rococo style in England, began
the landscaping of Kew Gardens and
was a notable collector of paintings –
both contemporary works and
seventeenth- century Italian and
Flemish masters. Today many of
these hang in the Picture Gallery at
Buckingham Palace alongside the
masterpieces acquired by his son
and grandson.

CHARLES WILD: *QUEEN CAROLINE'S LIBRARY AT ST JAMES'S PALACE*, in 1819. The wife of George II was the first patron of the Hanoverian dynasty, a keen gardener and book collector. Her library at St James's was a handsome room designed by William Kent (now demolished).

considerable royal patron by any standards, his early death (in 1751) has meant that his achievement has been somewhat underestimated. He and his circle pioneered the rococo style in England, partly in reaction against the Palladian architecture favoured by his parents and government officials. He helped to popularize chinoiserie in England and had a Chinese barge, rowed by Chinese boatmen, on the river Thames; while in 1749 he built an Oriental temple at Kew Gardens as part of a scheme for landscaping the gardens which fore-shadowed the architectural embellishments there of his son, George III. The Prince was an enthusiastic, discriminating collector of paintings, patronizing among others Italian artists like Jacopo Amigoni, who had settled in London, as well as buying Continental

DAVID TENIERS THE YOUNGER:
THE STOLEN KISS, c. 1640. This fine
work is one of a number of paintings
by Dutch and Flemish masters
acquired by Frederick, Prince of
Wales, foreshadowing the taste of his
grandson, George IV.

seicento masters. He appreciated Flemish pictures, including the
works of Sir Anthony van Dyck, Sir Peter Paul Rubens, Jan Brueghel
and David Teniers the Younger. *The Stolen Kiss*, a fine work by
Teniers of *c.* 1640, bought by Frederick, Prince of Wales, today hangs
in the Picture Gallery at Buckingham Palace. He also admired
seventeenth-century French and Italian painting, and acquired
pictures by Carlo Maratti, Francesco Albano, Pietro da Cortona,
Giuseppe Chiari and others. Guido Reni's superb *Cleopatra, c.* 1630,
and three landscapes by Gaspard Dughet, which hang at
Buckingham Palace, were all his. That Frederick's pictures were
given specially designed carved rococo frames shows the care with
which the Prince displayed his collection. In 1749 the antiquary

CLOCK DESIGNED BY SIR WILLIAM CHAMBERS FOR GEORGE III. This four-sided clock was designed by Sir William Chambers for the King in 1768. It takes the form of a classical temple with a dome and fluted Corinthian columns. The case is veneered with tortoiseshell and enriched with gilt bronze mounts. The mechanism was made by Christopher Pinchbeck assisted by John Merigeot and John Monk. The four dials show the time of day, a planetarium, the tides at forty-three British ports and the signs of the zodiac. George III himself is said to have had a hand in the design. Lady Mary Coke noted in her journal on 29 January 1768 : 'The case is magnificent, execution extremely fine, and the design partly His Majesty's, and partly Mr Chambers his Architect.'

LUCA CARLEVARIJS: *A CAPRICE VIEW OF A SEAPORT, c.* 1710. The group of paintings by Carlevarijs, Francesco Zuccarelli and no fewer than forty by Canaletto were among the 'modern' Italian paintings acquired by George III in 1762 when he purchased the collection formed in Venice by the British Consul there, Joseph Smith. This purchase was negotiated by the King's librarian Richard Dalton.

(*Left*) GUIDO RENI: *CLEOPATRA, c.* 1630. One of the Italian seventeenth-century paintings bought by Frederick, Prince of Wales, which now hangs in the Picture Gallery at Buckingham Palace.

George Vertue wrote that 'no prince since King Charles I took so much pleasure nor observations on works of art or artists.'

George III emulated his father in his love of the arts. He was primarily interested, as we have seen, in books, medals, architecture and the applied arts, but he also took great trouble over the arrangement of the paintings at Buckingham House. A plan of the hanging of the pictures in the different rooms survives from 1774. It shows how the King augmented his own purchases and commissions with paintings formerly in the other royal palaces, including two large portraits of King Charles I, 'The Greate Peece' of the King and his family, which had once hung in the Long Gallery at Whitehall, and the equestrian piece with Monsieur de St Antoine, which had once hung at St James's Palace. These are today among the most prominent paintings in the Picture Gallery at Buckingham Palace.

George III also bought paintings in Italy, despatching his librarian Richard Dalton to Rome and Bologna for this purpose. But the King's greatest coup was the purchase *en bloc* of the collection of Old Masters and contemporary Italian paintings and drawings assembled by the British Consul in Venice, Joseph Smith. This included over forty paintings by Canaletto, now distributed between

(*Far left*) SIR ANTHONY VAN DYCK: *CHARLES I AND HENRIETTA MARIA WITH THEIR TWO ELDEST CHILDREN ('THE GREATE PEECE')* 1632. This huge group portait of Charles I and his family was the artist's first commission for the King following his appointment as court painter in 1632. Originally it hung at one end of the Long Gallery at Whitehall. Today it is one of a pair of van Dycks painted for Charles I which dominate the Picture Gallery at Buckingham Palace. Most of Charles I's incomparable collection was dispersed following his execution in 1649, though some paintings (including this one) were reacquired by Charles II after the Restoration and still adorn the Royal Collection.

SIR ANTHONY VAN DYCK: *CHARLES I WITH MONSIEUR DE ST ANTOINE*, 1633. This balances 'The Greate Peece' on the opposite wall of the Picture Gallery. Originally it was placed on the end wall of the gallery at St James's Palace where it gave the impression that the King was riding through an archway towards the viewer. In this commanding image van Dyck emphasizes the royal status of the sitter, with all the trappings of a state portrait, and also pays homage to Rubens and Titian. Many of Charles I's van Dycks in the Royal Collection were brought to Buckingham House by George III.

Buckingham Palace and Windsor Castle, and the canvasses by Luca
Carlevaris and Francesco Zuccarelli, which introduce a welcome
dash of Venetian colour and light into the Buckingham Palace
Picture Gallery. The King patronized Zuccarelli directly, too, just as
his father had, commissioning, for instance, the huge painting of the
Finding of Moses, signed and dated 'Francesco Zuccarelli Londra
1768', which hangs in the Silk Tapestry Room. There are thirty landscapes by Zuccarelli in the Royal Collection as well as eight
architectural *capriccii* painted by Zuccarelli in collaboration with
Antonio Visentini which were bought with Consul Smith's collection. The *clou* of the Smith collection was not, however, Venetian but
the Dutch artist Jan Vermeer's *Lady at the Virginals with a Gentleman*,
still one of the masterpieces of the royal Picture Gallery. George
III also commissioned numerous works from contemporary artists
for Buckingham House and Windsor Castle, especially from his
Principal Painter, the American-born Benjamin West. The paintings
commissioned by the King from this artist for the Warm Room at
Buckingham House between 1769 and 1773 were of considerable

BENJAMIN WEST: *THE DEPARTURE OF REGULUS FROM ROME*, 1769. This was the first picture commissioned from West by George III and was inspired by the exhibition of the painting of *Agrippina Landing at Brundisium with the Ashes of Germanicus* which West had executed for the Archbishop of York and which the King had admired. *The Oath of Hannibal* was painted as a pendant to the Regulus. The seven paintings executed by West between 1769 and 1770 for the King's Warm Room at Buckingham House cost £2,100.

significance for the development of 'history painting' in England. The subjects extolled the virtues of bravery and magnanimity in different historical periods. The largest, *The Departure of Regulus* and *The Oath of Hannibal*, hang in the Cross Gallery at the Palace.

George III had little time for Sir Joshua Reynolds and commissioned no paintings from him (the twenty-three works by Reynolds in the Royal Collection were nearly all acquired by George IV), but he ordered splendid portraits from Johann Zoffany, Thomas Gainsborough, Angelica Kauffmann and the Scottish artist Allan Ramsay, the latter being responsible for the magnificent full-length Coronation portraits of George III and Queen Charlotte which adorn the State Dining Room. The Royal Academy was founded under the King's patronage in 1768 and he continued to take a close personal interest in its affairs.

(*Right*) SIR ANTHONY VAN DYCK: *THE MYSTIC MARRIAGE OF ST CATHERINE, c.* 1630.

BENJAMIN WEST: *THE OATH OF HANNIBAL*, 1770. One of the group commissioned by George III from West and intended to celebrate the qualities of leadership and loyalty. They hung originally in the Warm Room at Buckingham House. This large canvas is now displayed in the Cross Gallery. Benjamin West came to England from America in 1763 and secured the patronage of the King five years later. West's history paintings formed the cornerstone of George III's patronage of contemporary artists.

Following the illness of George III and the establishment of the Regency in 1811, the Royal Household was put on a new footing. Queen Charlotte was given an additional £10,000 a year for the upkeep of Buckingham House. At that time she began to hold her public drawing-rooms and receptions there rather than at St James's, and the first-floor rooms were rearranged and redecorated for this purpose. Heavily draped and fringed curtains of characteristic Regency taste were introduced, the furniture reupholstered in crimson and gold, and new carpets of Brussels weave laid down. In the Crimson Drawing Room, for instance, Elliott, Son & Francis supplied 'three pairs of scarlet embossed cloth curtains, cornice

BENJAMIN WEST:
GEORGE III, 1779

ANGELICA KAUFFMANN: *AUGUSTA, DUCHESS OF BRUNSWICK*, 1767. The princess was the sister of George III and married the Duke of Brunswick in Germany. This portrait was much admired at the time and led to the artist being inundated with commissions from English sitters.

NATHANIEL DANCE: *EDWARD, DUKE OF YORK, c.* 1764. The prince, who is shown in Garter robes, was the younger brother of George III, and the only member of the Hanoverian royal family to undertake a Continental Grand Tour as part of his education. He died young. This portrait was painted by Dance in Rome.

JAMES STEPHANOFF: *THE QUEEN'S BREAKFAST ROOM AT BUCKINGHAM HOUSE.* The black and gold 'japanned' panels embellished the principal first-floor room of the garden front of the Duke of Buckingham's house. Queen Charlotte had them repaired by William Vile in 1766 and repositioned here. Vile's bill for decorating the room amounted to £572 12s. 5d. The organ was supplied in 1766 by John Bradburn. It was crowned by a bust of George Frideric Handel.

etc' and 'two elbows, one stool and six single chairs with covers of embossed cloth' in 1810. Some of these chairs are now in the Blue Drawing Room. The Second Drawing Room, formerly the Queen's Dressing Room, was also hung with crimson cloth and given a large new looking-glass over the chimneypiece. The former Queen's Bedroom beyond became the Blue Velvet Room with light blue silk wall-hangings, lavishly draped velvet curtains and gilt ornaments in the heavier early nineteenth-century taste and a new carpet and rug were provided, the latter sporting the royal arms.

As redecorated *c.* 1812, the Queen's rooms at Buckingham House were transformed into a more formal suite for royal entertaining. They are recorded in this state in W.H. Pyne's *History of the Royal Residences*, published in 1819, a year after Queen Charlotte's death.

With its charming coloured aquatint illustrations, for which the original watercolours by James Stephanoff and Richard Cattermole are now in the Royal Library at Windsor Castle, it provides the best record of old Buckingham House before its sweeping reconstruction and aggrandizement by George IV when he transformed the place from the comparatively modest house which his parents had created into a glittering palace worthy of the British nation.

CHARLES WILD: *THE BLUE VELVET ROOM.* This was redecorated as a dressing room for Queen Charlotte *c.* 1812, in a Regency taste similar to Carlton House with heavy swagged curtains. The walls were hung with light blue silk and the chairs with matching velvet. The hearth rug has the royal arms.

CHAPTER TWO

GEORGE IV'S RECONSTRUCTION OF THE PALACE

'A Hash of Nash'

(*Previous page*) THE ENTRANCE FRONT OF BUCKINGHAM HOUSE, 1818. This watercolour from W. H. Pyne's *History of the Royal Residences* shows the building as it had been remodelled for George III by Sir William Chambers, with additional lower wings to the left and right. The vane on a tall mast supported by wires like nautical rigging was connected to the wind dial over the chimneypiece in one of the libraries below.

STUDIO OF SIR THOMAS LAWRENCE: *GEORGE IV, c.* 1820. It is largely due to George IV that Buckingham Palace has such magnificent reception rooms and is full of superlative treasures.

After Queen Charlotte's death in 1818 Buckingham House lay empty until George IV took it over for himself. Even before he acceded to the throne in 1820, the new King had conceived the idea of moving there and reconstructing it into what he called a pied-à-terre for himself. From his coming-of-age to becoming king, both when Prince of Wales and Prince Regent, he had lived at Carlton House at the other end of the Mall where the Duke of York's steps and Waterloo Place are now. There he had created one of the most beautiful small neo-classical palaces in Europe and filled it with superlative works of art. Carlton House was the overture to the King's larger project at Buckingham Palace, and many of the paintings, the spectacular English crystal chandeliers, the superb Regency and French furniture and even some of the marble chimneypieces now there were originally commissioned or collected for Carlton House. The State Apartments at Buckingham Palace are almost entirely furnished with the Prince Regent's purchases.

Begun in 1783 to the design of Henry Holland, Carlton House was constantly remodelled and redecorated in ever more opulent taste by the Prince under the direction of a series of different architects, artists, carvers and upholsterers until 1815. As originally furnished, the house reflected the fresh francophile tastes of the Prince in his youth, when he employed the Parisian dealer Dominique Daguerre to acquire contemporary Louis XVI furniture of exquisite simplicity and elegance. Following the French Revolution in 1789 and the systematic stripping of Versailles and the other French royal palaces by the republican government, he was able to buy the finest examples of earlier French royal furniture – Louis XIV Boulle, and ormolu-encrusted Louis XV rococo masterpieces, as well as the bronzes, marbles and rare porcelains and the Dutch cabinet paintings that went with them. Thus the Prince's tastes became ever richer and more opulent with age. In the early nineteenth century, whilst continuing to acquire French works of art, he developed a taste for English furniture based on antique sources with rich gilt ornaments and brass inlay, which today is thought of as characteristically 'Regency'. After the defeat of Napoleon I in 1815, he was able more easily to indulge his passion for French furniture and decoration,

SÈVRES POT-POURRI VASE À BATEAU. This bears the letter for 1758 and is decorated in green, blue and gold. The large quantity of Sèvres porcelain acquired by George IV reflects his unquenchable enthusiasm for French art. Many of these objects were bought after the French Revolution when the contents of the French royal palaces were dispersed. This vase may have belonged to Madame de Pompadour and was acquired for George IV in Paris in 1817 by François Benois for 2,500 francs.

CHARLES WILD: *THE CRIMSON DRAWING ROOM AT CARLTON HOUSE.* Some of the seat furniture supplied by Tatham, Bailey & Sanders in 1808–13 is now in the Blue Drawing Room at Buckingham Palace, and the gilded tripods with cranes are in the White Drawing Room.

continuing to buy many of the best examples which came on to the market both in London and in Paris. The greater part of the magnificent French furniture in the Royal Collection was bought in the 1820s. The Prince's constantly changing tastes and rearrangement of his architectural backdrops dazzled his contemporaries. In May 1810, for instance, Lady Sarah Spencer wrote after a visit to Carlton House that it was 'so magnificent just now – He changes the furniture so very often that one can scarcely find time to catch a glimpse of each transient arrangement before it is all turned off for some other.'

That old gossip and socialite Horace Walpole, who visited Carlton House in an earlier stage in 1784 when it was first being completed, left his impressions of its original appearance in a characteristic letter to his friend Lady Ossory:

FRENCH TABLE WITH *PIETRA DURA* PLAQUES, BY ADAM WEISWEILER. One of the most handsome pieces of furniture in the Louis XVI style in the Royal Collection. The plaques may date from the seventeenth century.

There is an august simplicity that astonished me. You cannot call it magnificent; it is the taste and propriety that strike. Every ornament is at a proper distance, and not one too large, but all delicate and new, with more freedom and variety than Greek ornaments; and though probably borrowed from the Hôtel de Condé and other new palaces, not one that is not rather classic than French… There are three most spacious apartments, all looking on the lovely garden; a terreno, the state apartment, and an attic.

The portico, vestibule, hall and staircase will be superb, and to my taste, full of perspectives;… Madam; I forgot to tell you how admirably all the carving, stucco and ornaments are executed.

FRENCH EMPIRE CLOCK BY PIERRE-PHILIPPE THOMIRE. This magnificent clock was bought by George IV in 1810 from M. Boileau. It is of ormolu and blued steel on a red Griotte marble base. The enamel dial forms the wheel of Apollo's chariot, while the wisps of cloud are a virtuoso piece of metal work. P.-P. Thomire was one of the greatest Parisian *bronziers* working in the neo-classical manner.

The 'august simplicity' of Holland's original design of Carlton House gave way over the years to a much more elaborate ensemble. In the early nineteenth century the ground-floor rooms were entirely remodelled by the architects John Nash and James Wyatt, a cast-iron gothic conservatory added to the design of Thomas Hopper, while the state rooms were lavishly redecorated with carved and gilded doors by Edward Wyatt and elaborate draperies, curtains and wall-hangings by Walsh Porter, a self-styled connoisseur and crony of the Prince, of whom an obituarist wrote: 'It seemed to be the study of this gentleman's life to crowd into a small compass every diversity of style.' Massive new furniture was

CHARLES WILD: *THE THRONE ROOM AT CARLTON HOUSE.* Four of the fluted pedestals with candelabra are now in the Green Drawing Room at Buckingham Palace, and the two council chairs by Tatham are in the Throne Room. Much of the furniture commissioned by the Prince Regent was moved to Buckingham Palace when Carlton House was demolished. This richly decorated room was one of the most magnificent of the Carlton House interiors.

ONE OF A SET OF FOUR GILT-BRONZE CANDLABRA BY FRANÇOIS RÉMOND. Of French royal origin, these came from the Cabinet Turc of the comte d'Artois at Versailles and were acquired by George IV after the French Revolution in 1820. They were made by Rémond in 1783. The corn motif was thought at the time to be Turkish and was described as *blé de Turquie*. The red marble bases with gilt appliques of griffins and lyres were added for George IV by Benjamin Lewis Vulliamy. Formerly at Carlton House, they are now in the State Dining Room at Buckingham Palace.

COUNCIL CHAIR, BY TATHAM & CO, 1813. This chair is one of a pair supplied by Tatham & Co to Carlton House in 1813. Today in the Throne Room at Buckingham Palace, they are among the most original pieces of English neo-classical furniture and were inspired by Roman examples of throne chairs, engraved by Charles Heathcote Tatham in 1799. Constructed in pine, limewood and beechwood, their finely carved backs and arms in the form of sphinxes are richly gilded.

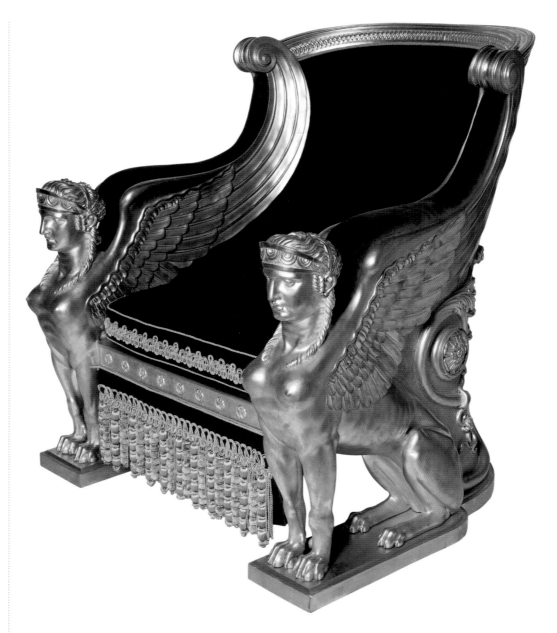

supplied to match by Marsh & Tatham (later Tatham & Bailey) of Mount Street, Mayfair, and vast glass chandeliers by Parker & Perry. In May 1806 the Royal Academician Joseph Farington had noted in his diary,

> Lysons said the Prince of Wales is incurring expences. Although Carlton House as finished by Holland was in a complete and new state, he has ordered the whole to be done again under the direction of Walsh Porter who has destroyed all that Holland has done and is substituting a finishing in a most expensive and motley taste.

With the establishment of the Regency in 1811, following George III's relapse into incurable illness, the Prince embarked on even more lavish schemes of furnishing, spending over £10,000 in that year alone, and similar sums over the following three years. Many of the large gilt sofas, classical *bergères* and other Regency seat furniture in the drawing-rooms at Buckingham Palace were all supplied to Carlton House by Tatham & Bailey and Morel & Hughes in these years.

Carlton House enjoyed its heyday in 1814 when the Prince gave a series of elaborate and glittering receptions there for the Allied

sovereigns, statesmen and commanders on their visit to London, during the Congress of Vienna. But after the final defeat of Napoleon I at the Battle of Waterloo in 1815 he began to lose interest in Carlton House, finding it, despite all the expenditure, too small, constricted and structurally unsound. Anticipating his accession to the throne, he began to think on a much larger scale, and to cast covetous eyes on Buckingham House, in its incomparable parkland setting, at the other end of the Mall.

Soon after Queen Charlotte's death in 1818 the Prince Regent informed the Prime Minister, Lord Liverpool, of his intention to move to Buckingham House, which he considered preferable in condition and situation to Carlton House, though, of course, a few additions and alterations would be necessary. Lord Liverpool warned him that building new state rooms would be unpopular, that Parliament could not be expected to grant any public money at a

SIR PETER PAUL RUBENS: *THE FARM AT LAEKEN*, *c.* 1618. George IV's purchases of paintings included several masterpieces by Rubens, of which this spectacular landscape was one of the most important. It was bought from the dealer Delahante in 1821. It is the earliest of three landscapes of this type by Rubens.

time of financial stringency; and that funds for building work would have to come from the sale of some other Crown property, such as the antiquated and inconvenient St James's Palace. Knowing how the Prince's building and decorating projects tended to get out of hand and exceed all estimates, Lord Liverpool also stipulated that the Treasury should have complete control of any new work.

The Regent let the matter drop for the time being but a year later, in June 1819, he raised the subject again, complaining that he had no suitable state palace. Lord Liverpool's stance had softened a bit in the interim and he now declared that £150,000 over a period of three years was the 'utmost sum' that could be provided by Parliament out of public funds. Any expenditure above that would have to be found from the sale of Crown property.

The Regent told his advisers that £150,000 was 'altogether inadequate' for the project he had in mind. Nearly half a million would be required: 'for the Building from £150,000 to £200,000 – for the fitting up, Fixtures and internal decorations the like sum – for Furniture £100,000. The whole expense may probably be kept within £400,000 but it will be safer to reckon upon £450,000.'

Nothing further happened for two years. But behind the scenes, outline plans and schemes were hatched at Carlton House for the transformation of Buckingham House. In July 1821, a year after he had acceded to the throne as George IV, the new King instructed the Office of Works that his favourite architect John Nash, who had re-designed the Brighton Pavilion for him, should be supplied with survey drawings of Buckingham House so that he could draw up plans for improvements. The original idea was to enlarge and refurbish the building as a private house for the King rather than a state palace. Nash worked at the plans over the next two or three years. The main block was to be retained but doubled in size by the addition of a new range of rooms on the garden side. The basement was to be raised, to improve the domestic offices at that level, the wings demolished and rebuilt on a larger scale on either side of an enlarged courtyard, the brick exterior covered in Bath stone and the interior, of course, lavishly redecorated. By 1825 the scheme had increased in scale and now included flanking pavilions or conservatories on the garden front, a triumphal arch – the Marble Arch – on the entrance front and the commissioning of an extensive scheme of external sculpture, partly to celebrate the recent victories on land and sea over Napoleonic France. The new palace was to be a national monument as well as a house for the King. The decision

was also taken to demolish Carlton House (rather than St James's) and develop the site to raise the additional sums that would be required to meet the inflated costs.

The new palace was to be the architectural climax of the 'metropolitan improvements' which John Nash had already devised for George IV. These included the splendid terraces round Regent's Park, the newly completed Regent Street and now Waterloo Place, the Duke of York's steps and Carlton House Terrace (on the site of Carlton House), a remodelled St James's Park with the new palace at its head in a characteristically English setting of landscaped gardens and triumphal arches.

Nash entered into the plans for the new palace with relish and produced a theatrical, francophile design which perfectly reflected George IV's personal taste. Despite the shortness of money and the need to retain and incorporate the existing struc-

DOUGLAS MORISON: *THE PICTURE GALLERY AT BUCKINGHAM PALACE*, 1843. This watercolour shows the Picture Gallery as designed by John Nash and completed by Edward Blore. The elaborate ceiling with myriad little glazed domes and hanging pendants shows the influence of Sir John Soane. The chimneypieces of white Carrara marble, which are carved with portrait medallions of famous artists, formed part of the large marble contract undertaken by Joseph Browne. The paintings were originally densely hung in three or four tiers, and included many bought by George IV.

ture, Nash rose to the occasion and produced a building which, for the first time since the destruction of Whitehall in the late seventeenth century, was worthy to be the principal metropolitan palace. Not that he was guided solely by his own ideas. The King himself and his band of artistic advisers constantly intervened with suggestions and alterations, and they were responsible for many ideas for the palace, including the internal planning, the scheme of external sculpture and the proposals for the decoration and furnishing of the main rooms.

The key figure in all this was Sir Charles Long, created Lord Farnborough in 1826, who was George IV's principal artistic adviser and the *éminence grise* behind all the Palace projects of the 1820s including the remodelling of the St James's Palace state rooms and the titanic reconstruction of Windsor Castle. Even before construction had begun at Buckingham Palace, as the King renamed the place, Charles Long had attended on the King in May 1825 to decide how all the furniture and works of art from Carlton House were to be disposed between the new rooms there and at Windsor.

Charles Long was descended from prosperous Jamaica merchants and was MP for Rye, Midhurst, Wendover and Haslemere successively before being created a peer. His principal interests, however, were artistic. He was a recognized judge of pictures and architecture, and formed a famous collection at his own house at Bromley Hill in Kent which he had designed himself on the basis of a preliminary plan by the prolific and versatile P. F. Robinson (a pupil of Henry Holland). Long also shared George IV's love of things French, and had had the opportunity to study Napoleon I's work at the Tuileries, designed by Percier & Fontaine, when he was dispatched by the British Treasury to Paris in 1817 as a commissioner, to settle the accounts of the Allied army of occupation. The Tuileries formed the major inspiration for George IV's new palace, providing a direct source for such features as the incorporation of panels of relief sculpture and the placing of a triumphal arch in front, based on the Arc du Carousel.

Charles Long revisited Paris on several subsequent occasions and some of these trips were on behalf of George IV. In 1826, for instance, he purchased Gobelins tapestries and Louis XV *boiseries* for use at Windsor Castle. Long was responsible for several of the distinctive features of Buckingham Palace, notably the extensive internal use of marbling and scagliola (artificial marble), which repeated the treatment at his own house where the hall and staircase walls were

marbled. The concept of a sculpture gallery on the ground floor with a picture gallery above at Buckingham Palace also seems to have been Long's idea; it differed entirely from the mode of display at Carlton House, but there was a similar arrangement at Bromley Hill House.

Drawings were being prepared in Nash's office during March 1825; and the following month the 'general designs' signed by the King were submitted to Lord Liverpool and the Chancellor of the Exchequer. These designs were approved and a bill was introduced into Parliament on 13 June 'for application of part of the Land Revenue of the Crown for a repair and improvement of Buckingham House'. In his typically slapdash way, Nash only submitted his estimate of the proposed cost a week later, and work had already begun on site on 6 June, before either bill or estimate had been submitted to Parliament. Four hundred workmen were employed on site. In order to meet the King's demand for speed, Nash divided the contract into three separate sections – one each for the main block and the two wings – each with its own contractors and clerk of works so that building could proceed concurrently. These initial contracts proceeded with commendable speed and the structural envelope was completed in just over a year.

As work proceeded, however, the King made endless interventions and alterations aimed at increasing the scale and grandeur of the new palace. In December 1826, after the structure had been roofed in, he decided after all that it was to be not a private royal residence, but a state palace where he would hold his courts and conduct official business, thus requiring a throne room and much grander state rooms. Nash half-heartedly pointed out that he had designed a private residence specifically tailored to George IV's personal wishes and requirements. There was no apartment for a Queen consort, and no offices for the various departments of the Household such as the Lord Chamberlain or the Lord Steward, who it had been envisaged would remain at St James's. George IV, however, insisted that it would 'make an excellent palace'. The need for some extra rooms was met by raising the newly completed side wings, which comprised a single storey and taller end pavilions, to the same height as the principal façade, thus transforming the Palace from a main block with lower flankers to a more solid U-shaped building all of the same dimensions.

By this time the government was beginning to worry about the increasing expenditure. The Duke of Wellington, who was now

CHIMNEYPIECE CARVED BY WILLIAM THEAKSTONE IN THE GRAND HALL. Inspired by the work of Napoleon's architects, Percier & Fontaine, this is the most magnificent chimneypiece in the Palace. It cost £1,000. George IV's bust and cypher at the top are a modest signature for the creator of the present Buckingham Palace.

Prime Minister, is reputed to have said, 'If you expect me to put my hand to any additional expense, I'll be damned if I will.' However, an extra £100,000 from the revenue of 'Woods and Forests' was allocated to the completion of the building. By June 1828 the expenditure account had reached £293,296 and a Parliamentary select committee was instigated to inquire into the expense of the Palace and other new public buildings then underway in London. Nash was extensively questioned but plausibly managed, at this stage, to convince his interlocutors from the House of Commons that all was under control. Their report merely commented on the 'regrettable necessity' for altering the wings and noted that 'other resources than those which were by law appropriated to it' were being devoted to the Palace. Rather surprisingly, responsibility for the accounts for the new building work was transferred, following the committee's report, from the Office of Works to Nash himself, just at the time when the ornamentation of the building, including the external sculpture and the finishing of the state rooms, was most likely to lead the King into initiating every sort of fresh extravagance. And so it turned out – with dire consequences for poor, easygoing Nash, who, following the King's death in 1830, found himself the object of a fresh Parliamentary investigation and censured for 'inexcusable irregularity and great negligence'. The hapless architect confessed that, 'Whenever I saw him [the King],

ANTONIO CANOVA: *FOUNTAIN NYMPH WITH PUTTO.* This was commissioned by Lord Cawdor and acquired from him by George IV. The Marble Hall at Buckingham Palace was originally conceived as a sculpture gallery to display examples of neo-classical statuary by leading Italian and British sculptors.

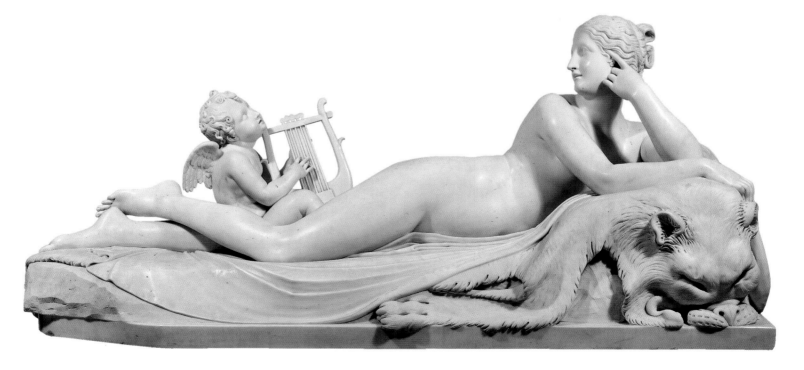

ANTONIO CANOVA: *MARS AND VENUS*, 1818. This was commissioned from the artist by the Prince Regent for the conservatory at Carlton House and now stands at the foot of the Ministers' Staircase at Buckingham Palace, where it forms an arresting sight at the north end of the Marble Hall.

CHIMNEYPIECE DESIGNED BY
JOHN FLAXMAN IN THE WHITE
DRAWING ROOM. Flaxman was the
leading English neo-classical sculptor of the early nineteenth century
and was involved in the design of the
marble embellishments of the Palace,
including the Marble Arch.

it generally happened that he ordered some alteration.' Nash was
sacked in 1831 for gross economic mismanagement. By May 1829 the
cost had already reached the staggering sum of £496,169, with the
building very far from being completed, and the Duke of Wellington
was demanding a 'Hash of Nash'. Now that the King was dead, there
was nobody to protect him from the wrath of politicians. The only
person who had been consistent in his idea of the cost was George
IV himself who had suggested £450,000 as a realistic sum for the
palace he had in mind.

The aura of chicanery and economic mismanagement surround-
ing Nash's reconstruction of Buckingham Palace caused it to be
scathingly criticized by contemporaries, more for political reasons
than for aesthetic ones. Though incomplete at the time of George
IV's death, the new Palace was, at least in parts, a building of great
originality and distinction, and it is the work of George IV and
Nash, even though overlaid by later schemes of lesser quality, which
still shines through today.

Nash doubled the size of the main block. This provided additional
sets of rooms on the garden side, grander in scale than the King's
and Queen's rooms in old Buckingham House, which were knocked
together to create the spinal Sculpture Gallery on the ground floor

GOBELINS TAPESTRY FROM THE
DON QUIXOTE SERIES. The four
Don Quixote tapestries in the West
Gallery at Buckingham Palace were
given to the Prince of Wales (later
George IV) in 1789 by the artist,
Richard Cosway, for the decoration of
Carlton House. Cosway himself had
been given them two years earlier by
Louis XVI. Cosway was among the
Prince's chief artistic advisers in the
1780s and helped to influence his taste
for French fashions.

SANCHO S'EVEILLE ET SE
DESESPERE DE NE PLUS
RETROUVER DON CHICRON
QUE GINES DE PASSAMONT
LUY A NDEVE

(*Left*) THE ENTRÉE STAIRCASE. (*Above*) DETAIL OF THE BALUSTRADE BY SAMUEL PARKER. Made of gilded bronze, this splendid scrolling design is a masterpiece of craftsmanship in metal.

and top-lit Picture Gallery above. The rearranged internal layout on the first floor permitted both a circuit of the state rooms and an axial approach to the Throne Room. The new rooms were thus equally suitable for formal audiences and for more social court events.

The key to the arrangement was the design of the new staircase (on the site of George III's and the Duke of Buckingham's, but completely rebuilt). It had a single straight flight, broken at a half landing where one flight continued straight ahead, providing access to an ante-room and the garden front drawing-rooms, while two curved arms returned to a balcony leading to the Throne Room sequence. The latter was of necessity much abridged from the traditional English palace state enfilade, comprising merely a small Guard Chamber, Drawing Room (on the site of Queen Charlotte's Saloon) and the Throne Room itself.

The exterior of Nash's Palace was faced in Bath stone. It was exquisitely detailed in a French neo-classical manner, making much use of sculptured panels and trophies, *oeils-de-boeuf* and carved festoons; while the principal feature of the garden front was a domed semi-circular bow, inspired by Pierre Rousseau's Hotel de Salm and Jacques Gondouin's Ecole de Chirurgie in Paris. Nash's design can still be seen in the garden front of the Palace, but the entrance front, facing the Mall, is now screened from view by the new east range added by Queen Victoria in 1849. Nash's great double portico, influenced by Claude Perrault's Louvre façade, has become the central feature of the inner quadrangle, while the Marble Arch, which was conceived as George IV's principal entrance to the Palace, was banished in 1850.

The Marble Arch formed a key incident in the sculptural decoration which was an important feature of the design of Buckingham Palace. This scheme of integrated sculptural ornament was intended to display contemporary artistic talent and was a reflection of the early nineteenth-century enthusiasm for British art, parallel to the commissioning of an army of marble monuments to national heroes in St Paul's Cathedral.

John Flaxman, the greatest of English neo-classical sculptors, was first approached to execute the carved decorations. He designed the sculpture for the Marble Arch and made some sketches for the other decorations, but he died in 1826 and so the work was executed by other hands. The Arch, which was made of white marble from Carrara, and modelled on the Arch of Constantine in Rome, was carved by Richard Westmacott and Edward Hodges Baily to celebrate the recent British victories over Napoleon I on land and sea. E.H. Baily was also responsible for the relief of *Britannia Acclaimed by Neptune* in the portico pediment. Other reliefs on the entrance front were carved by J. E. Carew, while much of the architectural ornament – including friezes, the capitals of columns, statues and trophies for the roof line, as well as the console brackets supporting the balcony and the friezes with stories of King Alfred on the garden front – was moulded in Coade stone (a type of terracotta invented in the eighteenth century by Mrs Elizabeth Coade) and supplied by William Croggan in 1827-8.

Nash and George IV are still the dominant spirits inside the Palace, where the principal interiors, though completed by other hands and redecorated in a different taste, are largely as conceived by them. The Nash state rooms are the principal architectural feature of the building. The richness of their fixtures and fittings distinguishes them from any comparable set of rooms in England,

ASTRONOMICAL CLOCK, BY JEAN-ANTOINE LÉPINE, *c.* 1790. George IV bought this clock, along with several others, directly from the maker at a total cost of £3,250. It was in the Royal Closet at Carlton House and is recorded in George IV's pictorial inventory of 1825. It is now in the Blue Drawing Room at Buckingham Palace. The tripartite design incorporates three dials. The central dial shows solar time (as would be indicated on a sundial) and mean time. The flanking dials give the date, day of the month, signs of the zodiac and phases of the moon. This is one of the few clocks in the Royal Collection to have retained its original movement.

THE OATH OF THE HORATII CLOCK, BY CLAUDE GALLE. This was bought by George IV in 1809 from Louis Recordon, the London agent of the famous French watch-maker, Abraham-Louis Breguet. Of gilded bronze on a green marble base, the composition is based on Jacques Louis David's painting *The Oath of the Horatii* and shows the three brothers being given swords by their father to fight to establish the supremacy of Rome. It was originally placed in the Crimson Drawing Room at Carlton House. Like many of the clocks in George IV's collection, this had its movement replaced by Benjamin Lewis Vulliamy in 1819.

and the originality of their architecture marks them out from contemporary palace rooms on the Continent. In their design they stretched the eighteenth-century classical tradition to its limits to create an aura of extreme opulence. Even those who criticized the exterior were enthusiastic about the interior, though some found the bright colours of the 'marble' and the elaboration of the detail a bit indigestible.

The plaster ceilings, in particular, were hailed at the time as something out of the ordinary, with their domes, and convex and concave coving. The forms developed out of Nash's Mogul 'tent' ceilings at Brighton Pavilion, and the eclectic classical ornament derived from ancient Greece and Rome, Napoleonic Paris and the Italian Renaissance. *Frazer's Magazine* commented in 1830:

It is indeed, not easy to conceive anything more splendid than the designs for the ceilings which are to be finished in a style new in this country, partaking very much of the boldest style in the Italian taste of the fifteenth century – They will present the effect of embossed gold ornaments, raised on a ground of colour suitable to the character and other decorations of the room.

Another particularly distinctive feature of the Nash state rooms was the incorporation of a wide range of architectural sculpture in the form of plaster reliefs. The idea of internal friezes in high relief may have been directly inspired by Percier & Fontaine's palace interiors for Napoleon I, such as Bertel Thorwaldsen's Alexander Frieze in the Quirinale Palace in Rome (installed for a visit of Napoleon's which in the event never took place). The key figure at Buckingham Palace was William Pitts, who designed and modelled most of the high relief plasterwork, including the tympana depicting the apotheosis of Edmund Spenser, William Shakespeare and John Milton in the South (now Blue) Drawing Room.

Pitts started out as a silver chaser and modeller, and had, for instance, executed the famous silver-gilt 'Achilles Shield' to Flaxman's design. His work has considerable grace and charm but is perhaps too small in scale to be fully appreciated in its lofty situation though it does, as George IV intended, add to the opulence of the decoration.

More interesting is the frieze in the Throne Room designed by the painter Thomas Stothard RA (who was also responsible for the design of the relief panels on the Grand Staircase) and executed by E.H. Baily. It depicts scenes from the Wars of the Roses -including

ONE OF A PAIR OF WINGED GENII BY FRANCES BERNASCONI. They hold up a medallion containing the cypher of George IV above the throne in the Throne Room.

(*Right*) THE THRONE ROOM.

68

DETAILS OF PLASTERWORK IN
THE THRONE ROOM. The frieze,
executed by E. H. Baily to the design
of Thomas Stothard, depicts the
history of the Wars of the Roses.

the Battle of Tewkesbury and marriage of Henry VII and Elizabeth of York – and is fascinating for its attempt to treat a medieval subject as if it were the Parthenon frieze. To the casual gaze it looks like a Grecian cast; only the gothic armour on the figures gives the game away. The same brave attempt to assimilate medieval ideas in classical dress imbues the bold display of heraldry in the shields of the four kingdoms of England, Scotland, Ireland and Hanover on the plaster cove of the ceiling in the Throne Room.

While William Pitts was responsible for much of the moulded plaster sculpture, the marble work was put in the hands of Joseph Browne, a manufacturer of scagliola. Nash sent him to Carrara to obtain suitable white marble and to oversee all that part of the contract. Browne was the chief contractor of the Marble Arch and was paid £6,000 between 1827 and 1830 for the chimneypieces in the Drawing Rooms and the Picture Gallery. Those in the latter were designed by Nash and comprise a set of five (one now in the East Gallery) with medallion portraits of famous artists which were almost certainly carved by Italian craftsmen. The other chimney-pieces were the work of a cross-section of English talent: Matthew Cotes Wyatt, Joseph Theakston, Thomas Denman (Flaxman's brother-in-law), R.W. Sievier, Richard Westmacott (Junior) and J.E. Carew. Browne also supplied much of the scagliola, and the inlaid marble paving of the Entrance Hall and Sculpture Gallery (where the Marble Hall now is) on the ground floor.

The ground floor rooms were deliberately low-proportioned and relatively austere spaces. The Grand Staircase provided a dramatic transition to the superbly decorated suite of state rooms on the first floor. Brilliantly top-lit from engraved glass skylights (reminiscent of the patterns in white damask tablecloths), Nash's clever manipulation of space was once matched by the richness of the finishes: polychrome scagliola wall panels (now, alas, painted white) and Samuel Parker's sumptuous gilt bronze balustrade, the rich Grecian foliage pattern of which is reflected in the design of the plaster string course. The unique mahogany-framed, mirror-plated doors were designed by Nash and, used here and throughout the state rooms, much enhanced the effect of sparkling spaciousness.

CHIMNEYPIECE IN THE STATE DINING ROOM BY MATTHEW COTES WYATT. This was designed with musical subjects for the Music Room, but retained when the room was completed as the State Dining Room by Edward Blore for William IV.

(*Left*) THE MUSIC ROOM, designed by John Nash. The parquetry floor is one of the finest ever made in England. The room was originally hung with yellow damask as a foil to the blue lapis lazuli scagliola columns (but later redecorated in white and gold for Edward VII).

DOOR IN THE STATE ROOMS. Designed by John Nash and covered with mirror glass framed with gilt metal mouldings by Samuel Parker, the doors enhance the glittering effect of the Palace interior. (A French eighteenth-century longcase clock stands in front.)

Other fixtures and fittings for the state rooms included engraved glass panes for skylights from Wainright & Brothers, elaborate ceiling plasterwork partly by Francis Bernasconi, and partly by Bullock & Carter, and the parquetry floors made of satinwood, holly, rosewood and tulipwood by Thomas Seddon. That in the Music Room alone cost £2,400. Though most of these were ordered by George IV and designed by Nash, they had not all been installed at the time of the King's death in 1830. In the event, these costly embellishments were to be assembled, the rooms decorated and furnished, and the exterior of the Palace completed by another architect for his successor William IV.

COMPLETION OF THE PALACE

Blore the Bore

(*Previous page*) A.C. PUGIN: *THE ENTRANCE FRONT OF BUCKINGHAM PALACE.* This shows John Nash's first design for the Palace in 1825. The old house has been recased in stone and given an impressive double portico, while low flanking wings terminating in pedimented pavilions flank an enlarged forecourt. This design was much ridiculed while under construction; the wings were heightened to line up with the main block and Nash's 'slop bowl' dome was removed by Edward Blore when he completed the Palace for William IV.

William IV, whose tastes were as simple as his predecessor's had been luxurious, disliked Buckingham Palace and did not wish to live there, preferring his own comfortable, smaller residence at Clarence House. He even suggested that the unfinished building might be converted into barracks. After so much money had been spent, however, the only sensible course seemed to be to carry on and complete the building either as a royal residence or as a state palace. The Prime Minister urged this as the best course of action. The question was who should direct the work now that Nash had departed the scene in disgrace. An urgent priority was to keep any additional costs as low as possible. At this stage the Tories, under the Duke of Wellington, had fallen from power and the Whigs, under the leadership of Earl Grey, had taken over the reins of government. The new Chancellor of the Exchequer, Viscount Althorp, and the First Commissioner of Woods, Viscount Duncannon (eldest sons of Earl Spencer and the Earl of Bessborough respectively) found themselves in charge of finishing the Palace - the Chancellor controlling the purse strings and the First Commissioner being responsible for architectural supervision, a job that was doubly important as the new king was so uninterested.

Althorp and Duncannon chose Edward Blore as an architect unconnected with Nash and the leading architects who had been asked for independent reports on the Palace by the parliamentary commissioners when they were investigating Nash's performance. Blore's recent rebuilding of Lambeth Palace gave 'fair grounds for supposing that he would discharge this duty in the most satisfactory manner'. He was appointed by a Treasury Minute dated 9 August 1831 and approved by the King the following day. The fact

SIR DAVID WILKIE: *WILLIAM IV, STATE PORTRAIT, 1831.*

that Blore's work at Lambeth Palace was unutterably dreary was beside the point; his reputation as a 'cheap architect' carried the day: after Nash's uncontrolled extravagance, the general feeling was that there was a need for less architectural brilliance and more financial control. Energetic and reliable, the son of an antiquarian lawyer, Blore exuded a dull competence, healthily free from any spark of genius. He was just the sort of man to appeal to the government officials responsible for overseeing the completion of the Palace. A sum of £100,000 was made available by Parliament for the extra building work.

Blore immediately began the job and spent time eliciting the view of the King, seeking guidance on the planning of the Palace from the Household departments and examining the fabric so far completed. To his credit he was appreciative of Nash's work and praised the 'number, magnificence, and excellent arrangement' of the state rooms, compared to which various practical defects such as the inadequacy of the basement domestic offices were comparatively trivial. The kitchen, for instance, was too small and damp. If the building was to operate as a state palace, many more rooms for staff would be required. Blore recommended building new offices and a servants' hall on to the south wing of the Palace and adding an attic storey to the main block to contain additional bedrooms. The latter, he thought, would 'unquestionably greatly improve its appearance' by giving him the opportunity to lop off the much criticized turrets and little dome with which Nash had attempted to create a picturesque roofline.

Blore stressed that he was 'by no means desirous of departing from his [Nash's] plans where I find it practicable to adhere to them.' This makes it difficult to decide how much of the finishing of the building is to Blore's design and how much is exactly as Nash intended. But we do know that drastic economies were made in the course of completion. For instance, the Marble Arch, designed as the main entrance to the Palace, was not finished according to the original scheme by Nash and Flaxman, its elaborately sculpted 'attic' being omitted. The carved reliefs by Richard Westmacott of Blücher meeting the Duke of Wellington at the Battle of Waterloo and the death of Lord Nelson at the Battle of Trafalgar, which had already been completed, were used instead by Blore to ornament the courtyard elevation of his new attic storey on the main block of the Palace.

The exact division of responsibility for the design of the interior

N. WHITTOCK: *BUCKINGHAM PALACE FROM ST JAMES'S PARK.* This engraved view indicates how Edward Blore altered and completed John Nash's design by adding the square attic storey above the portico, and the low screens, and guard house, on either side. The Marble Arch, conceived by George IV as the main entrance to the Palace and a national monument to the victories at Trafalgar and Waterloo, was designed by Nash and John Flaxman. Though all the sculpture had been carved, Blore did not complete it to the finished design and left out the tall entablature with richly carved friezes which was intended as its principal feature.

between Nash and Blore is even more difficult to ascertain than that of the exterior. Here Blore was merely finishing off work which was already far advanced and for which most of the fittings had already been ordered and executed at vast cost. The plasterwork of the ceilings of the state rooms was largely completed, and Pitts' plaster reliefs and Browne's marble chimneypieces were already in place, or in the process of being installed. Nevertheless Blore made certain revisions. For example, one of the marble chimneypieces ordered by Nash for the Picture Gallery was placed by Blore in the Ante-Room (now the East Gallery) at the head of the main staircase.

Blore's principal alteration to the disposition of the main rooms was the reconstruction of the Music Room as the State Dining Room, at the request of the King, who wanted a dining-room on the principal floor. The two marble chimneypieces, probably by Matthew Cotes Wyatt, which had already been carved with female figures playing musical instruments, were incorporated, but otherwise the room, its ceiling supported on restless bracketing and pene-trated coving, and with coarse plaster and papier maché mouldings on the walls sporting William IV's monogram, is almost entirely Blore's work, including the design of the gilt picture frames and large mirrors added for Queen Victoria.

George IV had intended to occupy the ground floor of the garden front as his personal apartment and some of these rooms had been designed as libraries with fitted bookcases. William IV decided to concentrate the royal library at Windsor Castle, and converted the Tudor wing of the State Apartments there into a self-contained series of book rooms. At Buckingham Palace the ground-floor rooms were completed as semi-state rooms in a simple late Regency style with plain marble chimneypieces and comparatively restrained plasterwork. The Household Dining Room, under the State Dining Room, was finished at either end with Ionic screens of white Ravaccioni marble columns ordered by Blore. In the Household Breakfast Room, next to it, the bookcases were converted to china cupboards.

New apartments for the King and Queen were created in the north wing of the Palace, connected to the Nash state rooms by an ante-room at the north end of the Picture Gallery. Blore also made a new garden entrance on the ground floor of the projecting north bow, the form of which survived from Chambers' additions to old Buckingham House. The main private royal rooms on the first floor of that wing were fitted with chimneypieces salvaged from Carlton House when it was demolished in 1827. Another sign of Blore's more economical approach was that the balustrade of the new private Stairs (later replaced by the Ministers' Staircase) was in white metal painted to look like bronze, unlike Samuel Parker's expensive real bronze balustrade for the main staircase, ordered by Nash.

As part of Blore's remodelling and completion of the private north wing of the Palace, one of Nash's three identical Ionic conservato-ries (all in the form of Ionic temples) was taken down because it blocked the ground-floor windows, and sent to Kew Gardens, leaving only the pair flanking the main garden elevation. Blore also added the low screen buildings with cast iron Doric columns and Coade stone royal arms, on either side of the main front of the Palace. That to the north was just a screen containing the garden gate. That to the south contained a guard room for the sentries on duty at the Palace. Blore hoped that these screens would overcome what was perceived as one of the architectural defects of the Nash design, namely the

THE BLUE DRAWING ROOM. Originally called the South Drawing Room, this served as the ballroom until the large new ballroom was added for Queen Victoria. The magnificent plaster ceiling was designed by John Nash. The furni-ture remains largely as chosen for the room in the reign of William IV including the sofas by Tatham, Bailey & Sanders.

too-narrow proportions of the pavilions at the ends of the wings. Blore was at pains to stiffen up the slightly cardboardy, theatrical quality of Nash's forecourt architecture. Nash was criticized for his stagey architectural bravura which worked well enough in stucco in the terraces round Regent's Park but, when carried out in solid stone as the principal royal palace, failed to convince.

Blore suggested inserting stone piers into the iron railings between the Palace and the Marble Arch as his first alteration to the Palace for William IV. He put his arguments thus:

The great defect of the East Front of the Palace is the want of an Architectural connexion between the Marble Arch and the wings: had the Fence instead of being of metal been constructed of stone with an Architectural character, the Arch would have appeared to belong to and form part of the building instead of being isolated and out of place ... The narrowness of the Wings is also a defect in the design of the front. Whatever therefore has a tendency to form a connexion between the Arch and the Wings and to give the appearance of a broader base to the Wings will as far as it goes be an improvement to the general design of the front: the latter object has been partly accomplished by the addition of the Guard House in the South and the New Screen on the North, and I feel quite confident that the stone gate piers will to a certain extent by throwing out something of an Architectural abutment on the opposite sides still more aid the effect, besides forming the Architectural approximation so much wanted between the Marble Arch and the wings.

The new piers designed by Blore were executed in white Portland stone. 'The colour holding an intermediate place between the white marble of the Arch and the [yellow] Bath stone of the building will harmonize with both ... and bring the whole of the buildings into connexion an object not undeserving of attention.' Whether Blore's adjustments to the Nash design for the entrance to the Palace were an improvement it is not now possible to judge, as all this side of the Palace has been subsequently remodelled and rebuilt. Some of Blore's Portland stone piers survive, however, incorporated into the forecourt screen of the Palace.

Most of the structural work was completed by October 1834 when the Houses of Parliament were destroyed by fire. William IV saw the fire as providing a good opportunity for ridding himself of his unwanted new palace. Sir John Hobhouse, a Whig politician who succeeded Duncannon as the First Commissioner of Woods,

THE WHITE DRAWING ROOM. The ceiling plasterwork was designed by John Nash. Most of the furniture and superlative chandeliers, here and throughout the State Apartments, were acquired by George IV for Carlton House.

noted in his journal for 18 October 1834: 'Went to St James's and saw H.M. I cannot say he was much affected by the calamity, rather the reverse. He seemed delighted at having an opportunity of getting rid of Buckingham Palace; said he meant it as a permanent gift for Parliament Houses, and that it would be the finest thing in Europe.' When he inspected the ruins at Westminster 'the King looked gratified as if at a show, and perhaps by the prospect of getting rid of Buckingham Palace. Just before getting into his carriage he called the Speaker…and said "Mind I mean Buckingham Palace as a permanent gift! mind that!"' In the event the government decided to rebuild the Houses of Parliament on their ancient site and held a competition for an architect for a new building there; William IV was left with Buckingham Palace, though he was, as it turned out, saved from having to move in by death.

Most of Blore's work to the Palace in the reign of William IV consisted of the enlargement and completion of the wings: the north wing to provide private accommodation for the royal family, and the south wing to create adequate domestic offices. The state rooms in the main block were finished off largely as intended by George IV and Nash. They thus represent late Regency taste in its most developed and elaborate form and, with the exception of the Picture Gallery, largely survive as the principal architectural feature of the building today. Though Blore was responsible for the completion of the structure, it is not clear who was responsible for the decoration of these rooms and of the arrangement of the furniture after George IV's death. The most likely candidate seems to have been Lord Duncannon, in consultation with Queen Adelaide, William IV's consort. It was her idea, for instance, that some of the silk damask for the walls of the drawing-rooms should be woven in Ireland to provide employment in the poorest part of the United Kingdom. But Lord Duncannon took the main decisions, guided by such notes and indications as George IV's advisers had left behind.

The furniture and works of art from Carlton House intended for Buckingham Palace had been stored in the Carlton House Riding School till the new rooms were ready to receive them. When George IV decided to pull down Carlton House, an inventory and valuation of the whole of the contents had been drawn up. In addition to this manuscript inventory, a pictorial record was made of the clocks, candelabra and some of the ormolu-mounted objects

COMMODE WITH *PIETRE DURE* PLAQUES, BY MARTIN CARLIN. One of the most sumptuous pieces of French furniture acquired by George IV, now placed in the Green Drawing Room. It has an interesting history. In 1782 it appeared in the posthumous sale of Marie-Joséphine Laguerre, a member of the chorus at the Paris Opera. The commode is thought to have been a gift from one of her lovers. The plaques were probably made at the Gobelins workshops in Paris *c.* 1680 by Gian-Ambrogio Giachetti, a craftsman from Florence. They were remounted in this extravagant confection of ebony and ormolu by Martin Carlin, one of the leading Louis XVI ébénistes.

from Carlton House, together with a few from old Buckingham House. Bound in three volumes and containing over 200 water-colour sketches of different items, this will have provided useful guidance for those responsible for arranging the state rooms. George IV had continued to buy things for the Palace almost up to his death. *The Times* on 1 March 1830 recorded 'some very splendid purchases have been lately made of furniture for the New Palace. Amongst them are a vase, which is said to have cost £14,000 and a cabinet, upwards of £7,000.' These prices must have been wildly exaggerated by report.

The Grand Hall, Staircase and Sculpture Gallery (now Marble Hall) were all finished to Nash's design and were largely the work of three craftsmen appointed by him: Joseph Browne, Joseph Theakston and Samuel Parker. Of these, Parker left and there was some difficulty in retrieving from him various models and details of unfinished items. Joseph Browne stayed on to work under Blore and to complete the contract given him by Nash. The halls at Buckingham Palace were his *chef d'oeuvre*, entirely lined in scagliola at a cost of £4,000; the Corinthian columns, the steps and the floors are of all white marble, the latter inlaid with a broad border of Siena and griotte marbles repeating the scrolling pattern of the plaster mouldings in the ceiling. The white marble of the floors cost £2,967 with an additional £968 for the inlaid work. The rich capitals of the columns and the superlative scrolling balustrade of the staircase were of gilt bronze made by Samuel Parker, who had previously worked for Nash and George IV at Brighton Pavilion. The balustrade cost £3,900 and is the finest of its type in England. Parker also provided the gilt metal mounts for the mirror doors, charging 7d. each for the little *fleur-de-lys* mouldings. The magnificent marble chimneypiece, the most impressive in the Palace, was carved by Joseph Theakston to Nash's design and shows the influence of Percier and Fontaine. The overmantel contains a clock flanked by winged victories and on top, above the royal arms, is a small bust of George IV surveying what was largely his personal achievement. Theakston was paid £1,000 for this work, which counts as his masterpiece. He came originally from Yorkshire, and had been an assistant to John Flaxman before transferring to the studio of Francis Chantrey, where he continued to work as a skilful marble carver. His contemporaries described him as a 'fine, venerable, kind-hearted man, ever prompt with a kind word and a kind smile'. He was much admired in his lifetime for his speedy workmanship and as a 'consummate master in making marble convey the qualities and surfaces of silks and satins, velvets and ermines'. Before his work at Buckingham Palace he had been employed for some years cleaning and repairing the monuments in Westminster Abbey.

The marmoreal splendours of the ground floor formed the overture to the state rooms on the *piano nobile*. There the elaborate stucco decorations had mainly been completed in the lifetime of George IV: the ornamental friezes by William Pitts, Thomas Stothard and E.H. Baily and the ceilings by Francis Bernasconi. Bernasconi

had been much employed by the Wyatts; he had worked at Windsor
Castle for both James Wyatt and Jeffry Wyatville. At Buckingham
Palace, in particular, Bernasconi executed the artist Stothard's
designs for friezes on the Grand Staircase. His masterpiece is the
pair of winged genii flanking the 'proscenium arch' in the Throne
Room. The Throne Room was finished under Blore's direction and
the scagliola doorcase – like those designed by Nash for the Picture
Gallery – was made by William Croggan with a little bust of
William IV on top recording the reign in which the rooms were
completed, just as George IV's bust in the hall chimneypiece down-
stairs marks the reign in which they were begun.

Joseph Browne supplied the scagliola columns and pilasters for
the three drawing-rooms along the garden front: porphyry for the
South Drawing Room, lapis lazuli for the Bow Drawing Room and
Siena marble for the North Drawing Room. These rooms were

CYLINDER DESK BY DAVID ROENTGEN, *c.* 1780. Severely neo-classical in design, this late eighteenth-century desk is veneered in finely figured mahogany. It is similar to one at Versailles made for Louis XVI in 1785. The interior of the desk is strikingly architectural with little fluted Doric columns and a frieze with metopes and contains a series of elaborate mechanical fittings.

gilded and the walls hung with silk damask in 1834. Lord Duncannon probably chose the hangings to complement the colours of the scagliola: crimson in the South Drawing Room, bright yellow in the Bow Room and gold and white damask in the North Drawing Room. The furniture in the rooms was also arranged in 1834, some pieces being brought from Windsor Castle to supplement those which had been reserved for the Palace from Carlton House. The Treasury allocated £55,000 for furnishing in 1834; Lord Duncannon retained responsibility for the finishing of the Palace even after he moved from the Department of Woods to the Home Office in that year. William IV was anxious to keep down expenditure on the rooms and worried that money should not be 'diverted to the Decorations, which he considers to form part of the Architectural Estimate, especially as He has never calculated upon the use of Buckingham Palace for any purposes of State'.

CABINET WITH *PIETRE DURA* PANELS, BY ADAM WEISWEILER. Seventeenth-century mosaic panels were reassembled in this ebony cabinet with Boulle marquetry and gilt bronze mounts in the 1780s. It was probably acquired by George IV for Carlton House in 1791 and is now in the Green Drawing Room at Buckingham Palace.

DETAIL OF *PIETRA DURA* PANEL IN THE WEISWEILER CABINET. The flat panels are of early seventeenth-century Florentine workmanship. The relief panels were probably made in the Gobelins workshops in the late seventeenth century.

ROLL-TOP DESK BY J.-H. RIESENER, *c. 1775*, made of oak veneered with purplewood and harewood with marquetry of flowers, a trophy of arms and a lattice design, and mounted in gilt bronze. This fine example of Louis XV furniture may have been made for one of the daughters of Louis XV at Versailles, like the similar desk in the Rothschild collection at Waddesdon Manor. It is now in the White Drawing Room at Buckingham Palace.

Duncannon, though sometimes wearying of his thankless task, continued with the furnishing of the main rooms. He did his job so well that many of the principal contents still survive where he placed them. The Green Drawing Room was provided with seat furniture from the large set supplied by Morel and Seddon for Windsor Castle c. 1828, and candelabra on fluted pedestals from the Throne Room at Carlton House. This room now also contains two of George IV's finest purchases of French furniture, cabinets by Adam Weisweiler and Martin Carlin, both embellished with panels of *pietra dura*. The chimneypiece was garnished with a pair of French bronze and gilt candelabra and the Oath of the Horatii clock, both

acquired by George IV for Carlton House. The chandeliers, here and throughout the state rooms, also came in the main from Carlton House, and had been mostly supplied to George IV by Parker & Perry c. 1811. They are among the most magnificent English chandeliers ever created.

The garden-front drawing-rooms were also furnished with a judicious mixture of furniture from Windsor Castle and former Carlton House pieces. In the South Drawing Room a set of four marble and gilt bronze side tables by Alexandre-Louis Bellangé, which had been bought by George IV in 1825 for Windsor Castle, seem as if designed for the room. They were in fact slightly too

THE 'TABLE OF THE GRAND COMMANDERS'. This extraordinary trophy was commissioned by the Emperor Napoleon in 1806 at the height of his military glory and was intended by him as a pendant to a second table depicting himself and his chief generals. It took six years to complete, and was presented to George IV by Louis XVIII in 1817. It was one of George IV's most prized possessions, and he instructed Sir Thomas Lawrence to include it in his Coronation portrait. He placed it in the Bow Room window at Carlton House. It is now in the Blue Drawing Room at Buckingham Palace.

large to fit between the bases of the columns and were reduced in size in 1834. The sofas and chairs in here include some of those made by Tatham, Bailey & Sanders for the Crimson Drawing Room at Carlton House c. 1810, and there were also some similar Regency armchairs from Queen Charlotte's drawing-room at old Buckingham House. The most important object in the room was one of George IV's prize possessions, the table of the Grand

THE TOP OF THE 'TABLE OF THE GRAND COMMANDERS' is made of hard-paste Sèvres porcelain edged in gilt bronze. It is painted with the head of Alexander the Great surrounded by twelve military commanders of antiquity, in imitation of cameos, displayed in a setting of simulated gilt and green patinated bronze.

Commanders commissioned by Napoleon in 1812 from the Sèvres porcelain factory with portraits of his generals in imitation of sardonyx cameos. It was given to the future George IV by Louis XVIII in 1817. George IV was so proud of this that he instructed Sir Thomas Lawrence to incorporate it in his Coronation portrait. It had formerly stood in the window of the Bow Room at Carlton House.

The Louis XVI seat furniture in the Bow Drawing Room at Buckingham Palace also came from Carlton House. The set was supplied from Paris by Georges Jacob, through Dominique Daguerre, for Henry Holland's Drawing Room c. 1786. The White Drawing Room was provided with French furniture bought by George IV, including a set of chairs by Jean-Baptiste Gourdin and a roll-top desk by Riesener acquired in 1825. Four gilt bronze candelabra on carved pedestals by Tatham, Bailey & Sanders had been supplied for the Crimson Drawing Room at Carlton House in 1811 but are perfect in scale for this room.

As completed, except for the State Dining Room, under Duncannon and Blore's supervision in 1833-34, the state rooms at Buckingham Palace were (so far as is known) faithful to George IV's intentions, and displayed some of his more treasured objects to great advantage. Indeed the magnificent furniture, chandeliers, candelabra and other objects probably appeared to greater advantage in the larger and grander rooms of Buckingham Palace than they did amidst the more 'flamboyant trappings' of Carlton House. All that was needed to bring the rooms to life was a resident royal family and the pageantry of court ceremonial. These were shortly to be supplied in the person of the young Queen Victoria following her accession to the throne in 1837.

J. Nash 1846.

CHAPTER FOUR

QUEEN VICTORIA AND PRINCE ALBERT

'A Total Want of Accommodation for our Little Family'

(*Previous page*) JOSEPH NASH: *BUCKINGHAM PALACE*, 1846. This romantic watercolour view shows the entrance side of the Palace in its final state, before the closing of the quadrangle with a new front wing and the removal of the Marble Arch to its present undistinguished site at the junction of Oxford Street and Hyde Park.

SIR GEORGE HAYTER: *THE CORONATION OF QUEEN VICTORIA*, 1838 (detail). In this picture Hayter captures the moment after the crowning when the peers and peeresses put on their coronets to the acclamation 'God Save the Queen'. Queen Victoria described it in her journal as 'a most beautiful and impressive moment'. The Queen moved into Buckingham Palace within weeks of her accession to the throne, and was the first British monarch to leave for her Coronation from the Palace.

The eighteen-year-old Queen Victoria shared none of her uncle's qualms about living in Buckingham Palace. Though she had some regrets at leaving Kensington Palace, 'for ever my poor old birthplace', she moved in to her new home immediately after her accession. On 27 June 1837 she was proclaimed Queen. On 13 July, with her mother the Duchess of Kent, she drove in state from Kensington Palace to take up residence at Buckingham Palace. Within forty-eight hours she entertained a large party to dinner in the State Dining Room and afterwards gave a concert by Sigismund Thalberg, 'the greatest pianist in the world…*J'étais en extase*'. On 10 May 1838, as part of the celebrations leading up to her Coronation, she held the first state ball in the Palace, in the South Drawing Room. In her diary the next day she wrote: 'I have been dancing till past four o'clock this morning.' On that occasion Johann Strauss (the elder) gave the first performance of his specially composed *Hommage à la Reine d'Angleterre*, a waltz which begins with a quotation from 'Rule Britannia' and finishes with an arrangement of 'God Save the Queen'. A month later on 28 June, Queen Victoria was the first British sovereign to leave from Buckingham Palace for her Coronation at Westminster Abbey.

The new Palace's role as a centre of the social, cultural and official life of the country was enhanced by the Queen's marriage in 1841 to her serious-minded German cousin, Prince Albert of Saxe-Coburg and Gotha. This set the seal on the use of Buckingham Palace as a royal family home, and a setting for large-scale official and private entertainment as well as state ceremonial and official business.

Prince Albert shared the Queen's love of dancing and together they arranged a series of costume balls in the 1840s, which allowed

EUGÈNE LAMI: *THE STUART BALL IN THE THRONE ROOM*, 1851. When there were a large number of guests the Throne Room was used for dancing as well as the Blue Drawing Room, until the large new Ballroom was added for Queen Victoria. On this occasion, the guests all dressed in the style of Charles II's court. Queen Victoria and Prince Albert liked fancy-dress balls.

the Prince to indulge his historical tastes, such as that in May 1842 at which the Queen and the Prince Consort appeared as Edward III (founder of the Order of the Garter) and Queen Philippa. Their medieval appearance on that occasion was recorded for posterity in a large, glossy portrait by Sir Edwin Landseer. The Strauss orchestra played again at the Palace at another ball in 1849 when the 'Alice' Polka was first performed in honour of Queen Victoria's six-year-old daughter, Princess Alice.

Music was not just restricted to court balls. The Queen gave a whole series of concerts in these happy years, and her favourite composer Felix Mendelssohn played at the Palace on three separate occasions, in July 1842, January 1844 and 1847. On the last occasion, shortly before the composer's death, Mendelssohn presented the royal couple with a piano arrangement for four hands of one of his *Songs Without Words*. Though not herself of a scholarly turn of mind, the Queen was happy to go along with the Prince's desire to have

SIR EDWIN LANDSEER: *QUEEN VICTORIA AND PRINCE ALBERT AT THE BAL COSTUMÉ OF 12 MAY 1842*. In the early years of the reign, Buckingham Palace was the centre of a brilliant social life with a succession of balls, concerts and banquets. Queen Victoria and Prince Albert appeared at the 1842 Bal Costumé dressed as Edward III and Queen Philippa.

'literary and scientific people about the Court'. Charles Dickens and other writers were frequently received at the Palace, and helped to leaven the official and political visitors.

In the early years of the reign, the South Drawing Room was used as a ballroom, and for very large entertainments the Throne Room was converted into a second dancing-room. Likewise for banquets, when there were too many people to sit down in the State Dining Room, the Picture Gallery was pressed into service in its stead. At a state ball in May 1852, both the South Drawing Room and the Throne Room were used for dancing, and the Picture Gallery for 'sitting out'; and supper was served in the State Dining Room at midnight. All the rooms were elaborately decorated with pot plants and flowers from the gardens at Frogmore and the supper room magnificently decked with gold plate (much of it made for George

DOUGLAS MORISON: *THE STATE DINING ROOM*, 1847. This room was originally intended by John Nash as the Music Room, but was reconstructed by Edward Blore for William IV to provide a dining room on the principal floor. The decoration of the room was completed for Queen Victoria, who hung here the full-length state portraits of her Hanoverian forbears.

LOUIS HAGHE: *BANQUET IN THE PICTURE GALLERY ON THE OCCASION OF THE CHRISTENING OF PRINCE LEOPOLD, 28 JUNE 1853.* When there were too many guests for the State Dining Room, the Picture Gallery was used for banquets in the early years of Queen Victoria's reign. The gold plate is some of that commissioned by George IV from the goldsmiths Rundell, Bridge & Rundell.

IV by the Crown goldsmiths Rundell, Bridge & Rundell). A contemporary newspaper described the 'Dining Room with a deep recess at the end within which a buffet was arranged on which the most exquisite specimens of jewelled and ornamental gold plate was most effectively displayed with the aid of a background of dark crimson and numerous lights from golden candelabra.' The tables were arranged in a U shape round three sides of the room and 'the service was entirely of gold plate'. Only 'single flowers of great beauty and groups of plants in full blossom relieved occasionally the gorgeous magnificence of the golden service.' The menu for such ball suppers generally included a large number of dishes – soup, pâtés, plovers' eggs, sixty or seventy entrées (hot meat dishes) and a variety of desserts including elaborate *pièces montées* or moulded sugary set-pieces. In case anybody starved a dozen different types of sandwiches were also provided.

Such court balls were attended usually by the royal family, the

LOUIS HAGHE: *THE NEW BALLROOM.*
The large new Ballroom added to the
south of the main block by James
Pennethorne in 1852-5 is the largest
room in the Palace. It was decorated
by Ludwig Gruner and Nicola
Consoni and strongly reflected the
Prince Consort's taste for early art.

diplomatic corps, politicians and officials and the English nobility,
and often by visiting royalties, most of whom were the Queen's relations. In June 1853, for example, the Queen gave a ball for the
Hereditary Grand Duke of Mecklenburg-Strelitz (the nephew of
Queen Charlotte, George III's wife).

In addition to these glittering but essentially social occasions the
Palace was also used in these years to entertain a series of foreign
heads of state, including Tsar Nicholas of Russia and the Emperor
Napoleon III of France. These were much more formal occasions.
Napoleon III was entertained at Buckingham Palace on 19 and 20
April 1855. The Queen described the dinner in her diary:

> *We dined at a quarter to eight in the usual dining room with all our suites.*
> *The Emperor, Albert and all the gentlemen were in uniform... The*
> *Emperor, as a matter of course, always leads me and always sits to my right*
> *... we two ladies sitting just opposite to each other in the middle.*

Official entertaining on this scale, together with the needs of a
family, rapidly outstretched the capacity of the new Palace. George

IV, who was estranged from his wife, Caroline of Brunswick (he had tried unsuccessfully to divorce her in 1820, and she lived abroad, mainly in Italy), had conceived the Palace as a grandiose 'bachelor pad'. William IV and Queen Adelaide, for whom the Palace had been completed, were an elderly, childless couple. Queen Victoria and Prince Albert, by contrast, had a growing family of young children and needed a different scale and type of accommodation.

The inadequacies of the existing building were already apparent by the 1840s. In a letter of 10 February 1845, the Queen wrote to remind the Prime Minister, Sir Robert Peel, of the 'urgent necessity of doing something to Buckingham Palace'. She pointed out

the total want of accommodation for our little family, which is fast growing up. A large addition such as alone could meet the case could hardly be occupied before the Spring of 1848, if put in hand forthwith, when the Prince of Wales would be nearly seven, the Princess Royal nearly eight years old, and they cannot possibly be kept in the nursery any longer. A

JAMES ROBERTS: *THE YELLOW DRAWING ROOM PREPARED FOR NAPOLEON III.* Napoleon III's stay at Buckingham Palace in 1855 was one of a number of successful state visits in the early part of Queen Victoria's reign. The Yellow Drawing Room at the south-east corner of the Palace was one of the rooms in Edward Blore's new range, and was partly furnished with some of the former contents of the Prince Regent's Brighton Pavilion.

provision for this purpose ought, therefore, to be made this year…A room capable of containing a larger number of those persons whom the Queen has to invite in the course of the season to balls, concerts etc is much wanted. Equally so, improved offices and servants' rooms, the want of which puts the departments of the household to great expense yearly.

The need to alter and enlarge the building went hand in hand with the reform of the running of the Royal Household. At the beginning of the reign, it was inefficient and excessively expensive. The organization, which dated back to the Middle Ages, was full of anomalies in its workings. The ground floor of the Palace came under the control of the Lord Steward, while the main rooms on

JAMES ROBERTS: *QUEEN VICTORIA'S PRIVATE SITTING ROOM*, 1848. The royal family's own accommodation formed a comfortable self-contained apartment in the north wing of the Palace.

the first floor were under the Lord Chamberlain. Though the Lord Steward had 'surrendered' the Grand Hall and other rooms on the ground floor, it was not clear whether he still remained in charge of the kitchens, sculleries and pantries. As Baron Stockmar, the Palace's *éminence grise*, pointed out in January 1841, 'more than two thirds of all the male and female servants are left without a master in the house…they may commit any excess or irregularity.'

Armed with Stockmar's criticisms, Prince Albert wrote to Sir Robert Peel in November 1841 pointing out that the Household was 'clumsy in its original construction and works so ill that as long as its wheels are not mended there can neither be order nor regularity, comfort, security nor outward dignity in the Queen's Palace.' The Prime Minister concurred, and soon after, Prince Albert's reforms, which still govern the running of the Palace, came into effect. The principal change, alongside a general cost-cutting (endemic in the Household like hedge-trimming in a garden) was the appointment of the Master of the Household as a deputy to the Lord Chamberlain, directly responsible for organizing the staff and domestic arrangements. The Lord Chamberlain was put in overall charge of the Household, while the Lord Steward (whose ancestry can be traced back via the Normans to the Frankish Emperor Charlemagne's court arrangements in the ninth century) was reduced to an essentially ceremonial role, attending the Queen on state occasions in the Palace, and leading the procession (walking backwards), with the Lord Chamberlain, to the State Dining Room when the Queen dined formally.

During the early years of the reign a number of relatively small-scale structural works had been carried out to the Palace, including improvements to the drains and ventilation, and the replacement of the small King's Staircase at the north end of the Picture Gallery with a more spacious arrangement called the Ministers' Staircase. In 1843 Nash's south conservatory was converted, under Prince Albert's direction, into a chapel. Nurseries and additional servants' rooms had been squeezed into a mezzanine and into the attic of the royal family's private residence in the north wing. In addition, Prince Albert started to improve the decorations and hanging of the pictures in the Palace.

He was a serious scholar of art, and in addition was a collector of early Italian pictures (some of which Queen Victoria gave to the National Gallery after his death). In particular, he was an admirer of Raphael and his sixteenth-century contemporaries. The Prince was keen to promote a revival of Raphaelesque mural painting in England. To this end he brought his own personal artistic adviser, Professor Ludwig Gruner, from Dresden to England in 1841; Gruner stayed in this country and worked for the Prince till 1856. The Prince built the Garden Pavilion by the lake of Buckingham Palace as a demonstration of his aims. It contained an octagonal room decorated by eight different Royal Academicians with frescoes illustrating Milton's *Comus* and Raphaelsque grotesques by Gruner. (Unfortunately it was demolished in 1928, having succumbed to dry rot.)

Inside the Palace, Joseph Browne's scagliola in the Ground Hall and Staircase proved defective and began to craze and crack. Deeming it incapable of repair, Prince Albert commissioned Gruner to paint over the walls with a colourful scheme of marbling and stencilling in an Italianate manner.

The obvious solution to the lack of accommodation at the Palace was to close the east side of the courtyard with a fourth wing and convert the building into a complete quadrangle. Blore was still the architect at this stage; he had designed the exterior of Prince Albert's Garden Pavilion as well as the Ministers' Staircase. Although it is clear that the Prince had a not very high opinion of Blore's architectural abilities, his reputation for cheapness and efficiency still held sway, especially as there was no money available for a new wing, and Peel did not think that the Treasury could provide anything. Peel was in the process of reintroducing the unpopular income tax (originally a temporary emergency to finance the Napoleonic Wars) as a permanent form of taxation; it was not deemed a good political moment for the government to be accused of assisting 'courtly extravagance'. The crisis over the repeal of the Corn Laws further postponed any architectural decisions. Nevertheless Blore went ahead, and drew up plans for a new wing with guest rooms on the main floor and smaller, private rooms upstairs. He also prepared estimates for the work, amounting to the reasonable sum of £150,000.

The Queen and her advisers decided to raise this money by selling the Prince Regent's fantastic Moorish-chinoiserie maritime residence, Brighton Pavilion. The Queen disliked the Pavilion because its urban site was too constricted and lacked privacy; she and Prince Albert were, in any case, embarking on a completely new, more secluded, seaside retreat of their own at Osborne on the Isle of Wight. The Pavilion was sold to the Brighton town council for

GRAND PIANO BY S. AND P. ERARD IN THE WHITE DRAWING ROOM. Bought by Queen Victoria in 1856. The Queen and Prince Albert loved music, and both Richard Strauss (senior) and Felix Mendelssohn played on various occasions, as well as composing special pieces for the royal couple.

£99,500 in 1846. On the assumption that the Pavilion would be demolished and the site developed for new building, all the Prince Regent's interior fittings, furnishings and decorations were completely dismantled and brought to London, where they were stored at Kensington Palace. Brighton corporation did not demolish the Pavilion but, on the contrary, repaired it firstly for civic purposes, and eventually restored it to its original brilliant condition as a Regency museum. The Brighton fittings, however, suggested a further means of economizing on the new wing of Buckingham Palace. Some of them were used, against Blore's expressed wishes, for decking out the principal interiors. As a result, the Luncheon Room, Centre Room and the East Drawing Room of Buckingham Palace are all improbable examples of early-Victorian chinoiserie.

STATUES OF PRINCE ALBERT AND
QUEEN VICTORIA IN THE GUARD
ROOM. The statue of Queen Victoria
is by John Gibson (1847) and was
originally tinted in lifelike colours.
That of Prince Albert, in Roman
military costume, is by Emil Wolff
and dates from 1846.

But they do not seem incongruous, for being originally designed by Nash and created by some of the same craftsmen as the state rooms, they complement the furniture and decorations of the main part of the Palace and provide a further reflection of George IV's personal taste. They add a welcome zest to Blore's pedestrian performance.

Blore's new wing made no attempt to relate stylistically or in its materials to George IV's Palace, which it unfortunately screened from public view. It also involved the removal of the beautifully carved Marble Arch to its present forlorn and unworthy site at the north-east corner of Hyde Park. Built of perishable Caen stone, the new façade sported an uninspired French classical style, somewhat reminiscent of an English railway hotel or, as some considered, a provincial German palace. It was altogether a dowdy performance compared to Nash's stylish, Francophile façades. The new front was not greatly admired at the time of its completion. The Builder, in 1847, remarked that it 'does not pretend to grandeur and magnificence, scarcely to dignity'. It was a lost architectural opportunity. Part of the trouble was the very tight budget; it was the product of palace-building on the cheap, something of which George IV could never have been accused.

The economies of building the new wing were, however, in themselves something of a miracle. Blore was able to reduce the actual costs to £106,600 from the original estimate of £150,000. This was partly thanks to Thomas Cubitt, who was awarded the building contract. Cubitt was the first of the large-scale building contractors. He had made his reputation developing the fashionable residential areas of Belgravia and Pimlico to the west of the Palace for the Grosvenor family, who were the ground landlords of that part of London. Cubitt had already built Osborne House for the Queen under the personal direction of Prince Albert and his reliable performance there decided the Office of Works to break with tradition and award him the sole contract. Blore considered Cubitt's prices to be 'perfectly fair and reasonable', especially as his costings for the carpenters' and bricklayers' work were five per cent less than expected. Lord de Grey (an amateur architect and member of the government), whom the Queen had asked to help superintend the additions, remarked that Cubitt was 'a very superior, intelligent person'. He had a lower opinion of poor Blore, who seems to have been depressed by the generally unenthusiastic response to his architectural contribution to the Palace and is

JAMES ROBERTS: *THE CHINESE BREAKFAST ROOM.* A watercolour made for Queen Victoria in 1850, showing how the fixtures and fittings from Brighton Pavilion, removed before its sale to Brighton Corporation in 1847, were incorporated in Blore's new rooms.

reputed, as a result, to have turned down the knighthood which was offered to him on completion.

The new wing and east front were completed in 1847. Thereafter attention turned to the 'larger room for entertaining' which Queen Victoria had requested. It was decided to add a new ballroom on a vaster scale than any of the existing Palace state rooms but continuing the principal enfilade to the south-west, with new kitchens below. James Pennethorne, a much better architect than Blore, was chosen to design this. He had been a pupil of Nash's and had completed the Regent's Park Terraces; it was rumoured he was Nash illegitimate son, though there is no foundation for such a suggestion. The new south-west block was built in 1852-55, again with Thomas Cubitt as the principal contractor on the strength of his favourable offer of executing the work on the basis of a seven per cent profit and 'on no account exceeding his total estimate'. The cost was £45,000.

The exterior of the ballroom takes its cue from Nash's garden front, being faced in Bath stone and adorned with Francophile details including sculptural relief panels by William Theed (Junior). Theed also supplied the carving of Hercules and the Thracian horses installed, under Pennethorne's direction, in the pediment of the Riding House (originally built in 1764 for George III) at the Royal Mews to the south-west of the Palace.

The new Ballroom was 123 ft (37.5 m) long by 60 ft (18.3 m) wide and 45 ft (13.7 m) high, making it one of the largest rooms in London. The internal fitting-up of the Ballroom and approach galleries did

FRANZ XAVER WINTERHALTER: *THE ROYAL FAMILY*, 1846. Winterhalter was Queen Victoria's favourite artist. His portraits immortalized the Queen and her family just as those of Sir Anthony van Dyck had done for Charles I. This large group hangs in the East Gallery leading to the Ballroom.

REMBRANDT VAN RIJN: *AGATHA BAS*, 1641. Bought by George IV in 1819 from the sale of Lord Charles Townshend.

not form part of Pennethorne's work but was carried out under Prince Albert's immediate direction by Ludwig Gruner and a team of artists. In its original condition it was a remarkable demonstration of the Prince's taste for rich Italian High Renaissance-inspired decoration, incorporating sculptural plaster reliefs, echoing those in Nash's state rooms, by William Theed and painted panels by a Roman artist Nicola Consoni after Raphaelesque compositions. Gruner himself painted the ceiling, putting into practical effect the theories he had propounded in his book on Italian fresco decoration. Consoni's panels on the upper walls represented the seasons. Consoni was a distinguished classical painter who had contributed to the murals of the Basilica of St Paul's Outside the Walls in Rome. Most of this decoration, alas, has now been effaced, but the original character and quality can be appreciated in the interior of the Royal Mausoleum at Frogmore, Windsor, which was also decorated by Gruner and Consoni for Queen Victoria as an expression of the Prince Consort's artistic ideals.

As well as introducing a serious 'artistic' note into the decorations of the Palace, Queen Victoria and Prince Albert made a significant contribution to the display of the paintings, arranging several of the rooms as dynastic portrait galleries and concentrating many of the greatest masterpieces collected by Frederick, Prince of Wales, George III and, above all, George IV in the Picture Gallery, where they were responsible for a completely new hang.

This policy was begun by Queen Victoria soon after she moved into the Palace, with the concentration of the full-length state portraits of the Hanoverian monarchs in the State Dining Room, all with the same gilded frames supplied by Ponsonby & Sons in 1840. The Queen was also responsible for the hang on the Grand Staircase, where she devised an array of portraits of her immediate relations which make a splendid display of late-Georgian portraiture, including William Beechey's portraits of her grandparents, George III and Queen Charlotte; George Dawe's of her father, the Duke of Kent, and her mother by George Hayter; her uncle William IV by Sir Thomas Lawrence and her aunt Queen Adelaide by Sir Martin Archer Shee; and Sir David Wilkie's striking portrait of her uncle the Duke of Sussex (and Earl of Inverness) wearing 'the costume of a Highland Chief', a picture which he gave to his niece in 1838.

No monarch added more portraits to the Royal Collection than Queen Victoria. An interesting aspect of her activity in this field was

SCULPTURED TYMPANUM by William Theed (junior) in the West Gallery.

LOUIS HAGHE: *STATE BALL AT BUCKINGHAM PALACE, 5 JULY 1848*, showing John Nash's Grand Staircase, redecorated by Queen Victoria and Prince Albert. Ludwig Gruner devised the polychrome wall decoration, and the Queen hung here a group of splendid full-length portraits of her immediate predecessors and relations.

SIR PETER PAUL RUBENS: *THE ASSUMPTION OF THE VIRGIN, c.* 1611. Bought by George IV at the sale of Henry Hope's pictures at Christie's in June 1816. The painting is an oil sketch for an altarpiece.

that she worked according to 'a carefully orchestrated iconographic plan', with different groupings of portraits in different rooms of the Palace. Apart from the Hanoverian kings in the State Dining Room and her close relations on the Staircase she arranged other sets of portraits in the ground-floor semi-state rooms. In the Bow Room, in the middle of the garden front, she inserted into the walls a series of specially commissioned oval portraits by Nicaise de Keyser and by (or after) Francis Xaver Winterhalter of members of the different European royal families who were related to her, including the King and Queen of the Belgians, the King and Queen of Hanover, the Grand Duke of Mecklenburg-Strelitz and other German princes. Winterhalter, who was introduced to Queen Victoria by her uncle Leopold, King of the Belgians, was her favourite artist and became her principal court portraitist. Winterhalter immortalized the

CLAUDE LORRAIN: *THE RAPE OF EUROPA*, 1667. One of George IV's finest purchases, it cost £2,100 at Lord Gwydir's sale at Christie's in 1829.

Victorian royal family in the nineteenth century, just as Sir Anthony Van Dyck had Charles I and the Stuarts in the seventeenth century.

Whereas Queen Victoria's chief concern was for portraiture, Prince Albert had a serious interest in Old Master paintings, which he nurtured under the guidance of his artistic mentor Professor Gruner. Together they initiated a record of the whole corpus of Raphael's paintings in the 1850s. Prince Albert rearranged the hang in the Picture Gallery, placing 185 choice pictures there and commissioning a catalogue of them from Thomas Uwins in 1852.

George IV had always planned to display his collection in the Picture Gallery at Buckingham Palace, but died before this was achieved. During the reign of William IV George IV's assemblage of

SIR ANTHONY VAN DYCK: *CHRIST HEALING THE PARALYTIC, c. 1619.* George IV paid the large sum of 3,000 guineas for this painting.

JAN STEEN: *A WOMAN AT HER TOILET, c. 1663.* Acquired from Delahante, 1821. George IV bought no fewer than seven paintings by Steen.

great Continental paintings, which was particularly rich in Dutch, Flemish and French paintings including masterpieces by Sir Peter Paul Rubens, Rembrandt van Rijn, Aelbert Cuyp, Jan Steen and Claude Lorraine, had been in store. All of them testified to George IV's magnificent sense of quality. As well as arranging these wonderful pictures, the Prince Consort also had all those in the Gallery framed identically. Once the disposition of the Royal Collection had been established, the Queen kept it as the Prince had arranged it, responding to a suggestion for change, later in her reign, with the statement: 'The pictures at Windsor and Buckingham Palace were settled by the Prince Consort, and the Queen desires that there shall be no change.'

The Prince was her lodestar in art and historical matters, as she later after his death somewhat deprecatingly told Sir Henry Cole, the secretary (the first director) of the Victoria & Albert Museum: 'she had no taste – used only to listen to him – not worthy to untie

his latchet.' The Queen was being unduly modest, for she could etch and paint herself, and had always taken a keen interest in paintings. But her tribute to her late husband's taste was not misplaced, for it was he whose artistic stamp was placed most firmly on the Palace in her reign.

His premature death, of typhoid fever, at Windsor Castle on 14 December 1861 was an emotional blow to the Queen from which she never recovered. The glittering social life of the Palace ceased instantly. The Queen herself withdrew to Windsor where she lived in a self-imposed purdah, coming up to London only for the day by train to conduct official business. The rooms brooded under dust sheets. The State Dining Room was not used for thirty years,

THE CAERNARVON ROOM. After Prince Albert died in 1861, Queen Victoria lived mainly at Windsor, and Buckingham Palace was shut up for large parts of the year. The State Dining Room was not used for thirty years and distinguished visitors, such as the Shah of Persia who stayed in 1873, dined in this room attached to the principal guest suite on the ground floor.

although there were still occasional family celebrations and state visits. Distinguished visitors dined in the Carnarvon Room attached to the Belgian Suite, the principal guest apartment on the ground floor, as in the case of the Shah of Persia in 1873. He was a particularly troublesome VIP. It was rumoured that he had sacrificed a sheep in his rooms, and it was certainly true that 'His Majesty generally dines alone, and when so, prefers to have his meals on the carpet...'

The late-Victorian gloom at Buckingham Palace lifted only briefly in June 1887 for Queen Victoria's Jubilee celebrations, on which occasion an enormous party of European royalties and relations stayed at the Palace, and the old glitter returned to the state rooms. As the Queen noted in her journal,

> *Then came the luncheon, an enormous one in the Large Dining Room which I had not used since '61. The King of Saxony took me in... Had a large family dinner. All the Royalties assembled in the Bow Room, and we dined in the Supper room, which look splendid with the buffet covered with the gold plate. The King of Denmark took me in, and Willy of Greece sat on my other side. The Princes were all in uniform and the Princesses were all beautifully dressed.*

Then the gloom descended again. By the time of Queen Victoria's death, at Osborne, in 1901 the Palace had not been redecorated, and the state rooms had hardly been used for a period of forty years.

CHAPTER FIVE

THE TWENTIETH CENTURY

'Not Internally Unsuited for its Purpose'

(*Previous page*) THE GARDEN FRONT. This survives largely as designed by Nash. James Pennethorne's Ballroom is on the right.

When Edward VII came to the throne in 1901, he found a metropolitan palace which seemed dark, dingy and very old-fashioned. He considered the immediate modernization and redecoration of the interior to be 'a duty and a necessity', as he told the Grand Duchess of Mecklenburg-Strelitz. C.H. Bessant, a now-forgotten decorator, and Frank T. Verity, the neo-baroque architect best remembered today for his theatre interiors, were both involved in remodelling and redecorating the interior of the Palace, transforming it in the process into a sea of white and gold. Nearly all Prince Albert's and Ludwig Gruner's polychromy was obliterated, as well as the remains of the Nash-Duncannon decorations.

Of these two designers, Verity was the more interesting and talented. He was the son of Thomas Verity, who had designed the Criterion Restaurant in Piccadilly, and had studied at the Royal Academy Schools before going to Paris when he completed his architectural training by studying at the Ecole des Beaux Arts and working in the Atelier Blouet, Gilbert, Questel and Pascal. Jean-Louis Pascal was a leader of the neo-classical revival in Paris, to which Verity took like a duck to water. On his return to London, Verity made a name for himself as a purveyor of a smart Champs Elysées style of architecture. His theatres included the reconstruction of the Imperial, Westminster, in 1901 for Lillie Langtry, a friend of the King's, and it may have been through her that he came to Edward VII's notice. Verity's work was, in any case, likely to appeal to Edward VII who was Francophile in all things to do with fashion and the arts of living, and who was personally involved in the diplomatic alliance between France and England known as the *Entente Cordiale.* He liked things to look 'Ritzy' – that is, rich, French and grand.

SIR LUKE FILDES: *STATE PORTRAIT OF KING EDWARD VII*, 1901–2. Edward VII remodelled and redecorated the interior of the Palace in white and gold, after long years of neglect.

THE BALLROOM AS REMODELLED IN 1907. This work was carried out for Edward VII to the design of Thomas Verity, architect, and White Allom, decorators. The impressive crimson throne canopy was designed by Sir Edwin Lutyens and was made out of the imperial shamiana used at the Delhi Durbar in 1911. The Ballroom is, today, the setting for state banquets and investitures.

Verity's major work at the Palace was the thorough remodelling of Queen Victoria and Prince Albert's Ballroom in a *beaux-arts* Louis XVI manner with fluted Ionic pilasters, *oeil-de-boeuf* windows and framed Gobelins tapestries on the walls. The designs for this were begun in 1904. Sir Albert Richardson, who started his architectural career as Verity's assistant, recalled being sent to the Palace to make a survey of the room preparatory to drawing up new plans and 'making his way through piles of discarded furniture that had belonged to Queen Victoria and which the King was anxious to throw out'. The work itself was executed in 1907, after a more 'powerful and elastic system' for heating and ventilating had been installed. The contractors were the then well-known firm of

Mayfair decorators White Allom, who were paid £8,145 4s. 5d. for their work. It may be that they modified Verity's design in the execution. Certainly, the room as finished differed somewhat from Verity's design of 1904. The most theatrical feature of the room, the great crimson throne canopy, was a later insertion. It was designed by Sir Edwin Lutyens for the Delhi Durbar in 1911.

White Allom continued to be employed on redecorating the Palace throughout Edward VII's reign and into the next. Almost as drastic as the reconstruction of the Ballroom was the redecoration of the Grand Hall, Grand Staircase and Marble Hall. C.H. Bessant of the firm of Bertram & Son was employed to do this in 1902-3. Bessant added incongruous carved wooden swags and finicky plaster panels, and painted over all Gruner's polychromy in white with heavily gilt details. The result was at odds with the more restrained, marmoreal character of Nash's architecture and perhaps more in tune with the luxury hotels which were such a feature of Edwardian London. The use of firms of commercial decorators, like White Allom or Bertram's, to do work hitherto the preserve of architects, artists and sculptors reflects the conventional taste of fashionable London at that period, when a tidal wave of white and gold swept through Mayfair and Belgravia.

As well as redecorating the Palace, Edward VII also cleaned and repaired many of the works of art. Almost immediately after succeeding, on 5 March 1901 he appointed Lionel Cust as Surveyor of pictures. Cust found the paintings darkened by discoloured varnish and fumes from the gaslights. He tells in his memoirs how when the top level of paintings in the Gallery were taken down they were 'found in parts to be coated with a thin dark film of dirt in some cases amounting to opaque black'. Many of them were cleaned by F.M. Haines and Prince Albert's hang was sweepingly changed, the King himself, as Cust recorded, 'enjoying nothing so much in the intervals of leisure as sitting in a roomful of workmen and giving directions in person'. Edward VII freely admitted that he was prepared to be guided by others in the details of artistic taste but he had an eye for the way things were displayed. He told Cust (rolling his r's in characteristic fashion): 'I do not know much about Arrt but I think I know something about Arr-r- angement.'

The general intention was to create a magnificent effect as a background to a glittering court life which surpassed even that of Queen Victoria's early years in splendour. The King, and his consort Queen Alexandra, were determined to revive the high standards of

THE BALCONY, which has become something of a national institution, was part of Edward Blore's design for the east front. It was first used by Queen Victoria to see off the Guards' regiments to the Crimean War. It was part of the specification for Sir Aston Webb's redesign that the balcony should be retained to the same scale as before.

royal entertaining and aimed to make the meals served at the Palace the best in the world. The tone was set by the Coronation Banquet in August 1902, which comprised no fewer than fourteen courses including sturgeon, lobster, caviare, quails and *foie gras*. Throughout Edward VII's reign the Palace formed the undisputed focus of fashionable social life in London.

Some atonement for the rather philistine Edwardian alterations to the interior of the Palace was made by the work carried out at Buckingham Palace in the next reign, under King George V and Queen Mary. The Queen had a considerable knowledge of furniture and decoration and was among the earlier enthusiasts for the Georgian and Regency periods. As she remarked, 'many things were changed here and at Windsor much too quickly by our predecessors', and she set about restoring more of a Regency character to the rooms.

The major external change to the Palace was the complete

THE PRINCIPAL FAÇADE AND
QUEEN VICTORIA MEMORIAL.
Edward Blore's east wing was totally
refaced in Portland stone to the
design of Sir Aston Webb in 1913 as
part of the Queen Victoria Memorial.
The Memorial included the remod-
elling of the Mall, the Admiralty
Arch and the *rond point* in front of the
Palace with the large statue of the
Queen-Empress by Thomas Brock.

remodelling of the Blore east wing. Blore had used a perishable
Caen stone from France for his building which rapidly deteriorated
in the sooty London climate and had to be painted (as his surviving
quadrangle elevation still is). It was therefore decided in 1913 to
reface the Blore front in Portland stone to a new design, as a backdrop to the Queen Victoria Memorial and the culmination of the
remodelled approach along the Mall planned in 1901. The work was
done with almost military precision and speed in under thirteen
weeks, without even breaking the glass in the existing windows. The
royal family had expected it to take a whole year, and were greatly
relieved at this minimum disturbance.

The deterioration of Blore's stonework had provided the excuse
for remodelling the façade, but equally strong was the feeling that
it was not up to the standard of many of the magnificent new public
buildings being constructed of Portland stone in Edwardian London.
As Lord Harcourt, the First Commissioner of Works, told
Parliament in 1910, 'Buckingham Palace is not internally unsuited for
its purpose, but I should be glad if I had the opportunity and the
money to reface it on its Eastern front.' By a happy turn, the funds
raised for the Queen Victoria Memorial were found to be in surplus
and this provided the necessary money of about £60,000 for the new
Palace façade.

Sir Aston Webb, the most prolific architect of public buildings in
the United Kingdom and a master of architectural pomp and

SIR LUKE FILDES: *STATE PORTRAIT OF KING GEORGE V*, 1911–12. In George V's reign the Palace was refronted and the Picture Gallery remodelled.

SIR WILLIAM LLEWELLYN: *STATE PORTRAIT OF QUEEN MARY*, 1911–13. Queen Mary took a great interest in the Royal Collection, rearranging furniture and pictures and adding appropriate pieces acquired by herself.

circumstance, responsible for, among other massive projects, the new Victoria & Albert Museum buildings in South Kensington and Birmingham University, had won the competition in 1901 for the Queen Victoria Memorial with a scheme for replanning the Mall and a large statue by Thomas Brock in front of the Palace. The Admiralty Arch at the east end of the Mall, opening into Trafalgar Square, had already been designed by Webb satisfactorily and completed in 1911, and so he was commissioned to design the new façade. George V trimmed various bits of excess ornament from Webb's design, and made sure that the central balcony was not 'curtailed as it is used from time to time on occasions when the King and other members of the Royal Family wish to show themselves to the people'. The result is a handsome, restrained, classical façade which shows the influence of Louis XVI's architect Jacques Gabriel's façades in the Place de la Concorde in Paris. Its dignified, self-assured appearance is perfectly adapted to its purpose, and it is due to Aston Webb that Buckingham Palace today looks like every child's idea of a Palace. The gleaming white of the Portland stone provides a perfect backdrop to the red tunics of the sentries on duty. Much of the grand effect comes from the forecourt with its magnificent new gateways and gilded iron railings. Some of the carved stone piers are Blore's for William IV and Edward Wyatt's for George III, but the principal gates were all designed by Webb. The splendid ironwork was made by the Bromsgrove Guild and is signed by Gilbert and Weingartner. The locks with little cherubs clambering round the keyholes are easily overlooked, but are charming little works of art in themselves. The whole of the new façade, forecourt and processional approaches were completed by the outbreak of the First World War in 1914.

The outside completed, attention was turned to the inside of the Palace, where a major architectural alteration took place in the Picture Gallery in 1914. As designed by Nash, the Gallery was provided with top-lighting through an ingenious part-glazed timber ceiling composed of hammerbeams with pendant arches and seventeen little saucer domes. The complicated design of this owed something to the example of Nash's rival, Sir John Soane, in his own home in Lincoln's Inn Fields (which survives as a museum). This ceiling, however, had always been deemed impractical. It leaked, as well as failing to throw light properly on to the pictures, and it had already been modified slightly by Blore. In 1914 it was totally replaced by a new segmental glazed ceiling and a deep plaster frieze

THE CENTRE ROOM windows give access to the balcony overlooking the Queen Victoria Memorial and the Mall. Here the Royal Family appears on special occasions.

DETAIL OF THE FORECOURT GATES, 1914. These magnificent examples of ironworkers' craft bordering on sculpture were executed by the Bromsgrove Guild.

with floral swags. The doorcases were also replaced, and the colum-
nar screen at the south end redesigned. The Nash doorcases,
supplied by Croggan, had been of white scagliola with flanking
caryatid figures. The new doorcases were of dark wood with carv-
ings in the style of Grinling Gibbons made by H.H. Martyn of
Cheltenham. The architect was Frank Baines, the Chief Architect
to the Board of Works. The general style of the room is vaguely
seventeenth century in feel. The result is, however, rather like the
saloon of one of the great ocean liners of the period. Its 'subdued
tastefulness' seems strangely at odds with the extreme opulence of
Nash's adjoining drawing-rooms. The walls were hung in 1914 with
olive-green silk damask woven by Warners and based on an old

THE PICTURE GALLERY. The ceiling
was rebuilt, the doorcases redesigned
and the deep plaster frieze added as
part of a thorough-going remodelling
in 1914 for George V. The work was
carried out under the direction of
Frank Baines, chief architect of the
Office of Works. Its 'restrained tastefulness' contrasts with the lavish
opulence of the Nash state rooms.

example at Welbeck Abbey in Nottinghamshire, the seat of the Dukes of Portland (since replaced in a different colour). The King disliked gold walls and 'both Their Majesties favoured green'.

The hang of the paintings was once again rearranged by Lionel Cust, to create a perfectly symmetrical, though still dense and formal, hang in the tradition of Palace rooms since the sixteenth century.

Queen Mary took a keen personal interest in the interiors of all the royal palaces and initiated many improvements and schemes of restoration. At Buckingham Palace she carried out a great deal of redecoration and rearrangement of the furniture. The Chinese decoration of some of Blore's rooms was also enhanced under the direction of Sir Charles Allom, the smart decorator, especially the Centre Room and Yellow Drawing Room, where old Chinese wall-papers and silk hangings found in store were installed. They had probably been bought originally by George IV for the Brighton Pavilion. New guest suites were contrived for important visitors and furnished partly with new acquisitions of English Georgian and Regency furniture carefully chosen to complement the existing royal collections. Perhaps Queen Mary's greatest contribution to Buckingham Palace was the rearrangement and restoration of

ONE OF A PAIR OF BLACK SÈVRES PORCELAIN VASES, *c.* 1790–2, painted in platinum and gold on a black ground with chinoiserie scenes and with gilt bronze mounts.

THE CHINESE DINING ROOM.
One of a number of unlikely early
Victorian Chinese rooms in the east
wing of Buckingham Palace, made
for Queen Victoria out of the
salvaged fittings and furnishings
from George IV's Brighton Pavilion.
The chinoiserie was enhanced for
Queen Mary by the decorators
White Allom in the 1920s.

historic contents, reassembling sets of chairs, for instance, which
had been split up. The informed and historically accurate approach,
initiated by Queen Mary, has conditioned the upkeep and presen-
tation of the royal residences and their contents down to the
present. Queen Mary was assisted by Clifford Smith, the Keeper of
Furniture at the Victoria & Albert Museum, and she commissioned
from him a detailed history of the building and its contents
(*Buckingham Palace*, published by *Country Life* in 1931) which is still the
standard work on the subject.

Under King George VI and Queen Elizabeth, little was done to
the Palace as the outbreak of the Second World War coincided with
the first half of the King's reign. During the war, the royal family,

PAINTED CHINOISERIE PANEL BY
ROBERT JONES from a set originally
commissioned by George IV for the
Banqueting Room of Brighton
Pavilion. Some were reused by
Queen Victoria in the Chinese
Dining Room, and others placed by
Queen Mary in the Centre Room.

including the two young Princesses Elizabeth and Margaret, spent much of the time at Windsor Castle. The Palace was damaged by bombs but fortunately no major features were destroyed. The worst casualty was the Victorian private chapel in the south-west pavil-

STATUE OF MRS JORDAN BY SIR
FRANCIS CHANTREY, 1834. This was
bequeathed to H.M. The Queen by
the Earl of Munster, a descendant of
Mrs Jordan and William IV. It is
displayed in the lobby to the Silk
Tapestry Room.

THE GREEN DRAWING ROOM,
showing the modern silk hangings
on the walls. The seat furniture is
part of a large set commissioned
from Morel & Seddon by George IV
for Windsor Castle.

ion on the garden front. This was reconstructed in 1962 as a modern
top-lit art gallery for the display of changing exhibitions drawn
from the Royal Collection, called The Queen's Gallery. This is open
for most of the year, while the state rooms themselves have been
opened to the public in the late summer, when The Queen is at
Balmoral Castle, since 1993.

Today The Queen and the Duke of Edinburgh live in the private
apartments on the north side of the Palace; rooms on the upper
floors of the north and east sides are occupied by other members

THE MECKLENBURG SERVICE, 1763.
This large rococo service, painted in
blue and gold with naturalistic birds
and flowers, was commissioned from
the Chelsea factory by George III
and Queen Charlotte in 1763 and
given as a present to the latter's
brother, Duke Adolphus Frederick
IV of Mecklenburg-Strelitz. It
remained in the ducal collection
until 1919. It was presented to
Queen Elizabeth in 1947, and is now
displayed in cases in the Bow Room
on the ground floor of the west wing.

BOOKCASE MADE BY WILLIAM VILE, FOR BUCKINGHAM HOUSE, 1762. This magnificent piece of English eighteenth-century furniture was acquired for the Royal Collection by Queen Mary in whose family (the Tecks, Dukes of Cambridge) it had descended. It was made for Queen Charlotte and formed part of the original furnishings of Buckingham House. Of strongly architectural form, with a broken pediment and Corinthian columns, it is magnificently executed in carved mahogany.

of the royal family. Much of the ground floor and the south wing of the Palace is occupied by Household officials and service quarters. The principal rooms which still form the backdrop to the pageantry of court ceremonial and official entertaining occupy the main west block facing the gardens. In all, Buckingham Palace has 19 state rooms, 52 royal and guest bedrooms, 188 staff bedrooms, 92 offices and 78 bathrooms. Some 450 people work in the Palace and 40,000 people are entertained there every year.

Unlike many other historic monuments, Buckingham Palace remains a fully occupied, working royal palace, which gives it a particular fascination. The Queen, as head of state, receives there a large number of formal and informal visitors, including the Prime Minister at weekly audiences, the Privy Council, foreign and British ambassadors and high commissioners, bishops, senior officers of the armed services and the civil service. There are regular investitures in the Ballroom. Each year in the autumn The Queen gives a splendid formal reception in the state rooms for all the diplomatic corps in London. Three times a year, in the summer,

WATERLOO VASE AND ADMIRALTY
TEMPLE IN THE GARDEN. The
gardens at Buckingham Palace are
one of its most attractive features.
They were laid out for George IV by
William Townsend Aiton, the head
gardener from Kew. Some embellishments have been added in this
century including the Palladian
temple, attributed to John Vardy,
originally from the garden of
Admiralty House and moved here in
the 1890s, and Richard Westmacott's
Waterloo Vase given to the National
Gallery by William IV but returned
here in 1906. It was carved out of a
single block of marble chosen by
Napoleon but given to George IV
by the Duke of Tuscany. It weighs
twenty tons.

garden parties are held, attended by a wide range of guests, includ-ing MPs, clergy and those active in local and public life, amounting to 27,000 people in all. An innovation of the present reign are the small private lunch parties for special guests from public life given by The Queen and the Duke of Edinburgh. The highlight of royal entertaining, however, is the state banquet, usually for about 170 guests, given by The Queen on the evening of the first day of a state visit of a foreign head of state to the United Kingdom. At Buckingham Palace, state banquets are held in the Ballroom, the largest of the state rooms, which is specially decorated for the occa-sion with flowers from the royal gardens and magnificent gold plate from the Royal Collection, much of it made for George IV. Guests are received in the Music Room and after they have taken their places at table a royal procession is formed to the Ballroom, led by The Queen and the visiting head of state and preceded by the Lord Chamberlain and the Lord Steward, who both walk backwards.

The Lord Chamberlain is the head of the whole household orga-nization of the Palace and responsible for court ceremonial as well as the upkeep of the building and its collections, and the day-to-day running of the Palace. Under him are seven heads of departments: the Private Secretary; the Crown Equerry, in charge of the Mews; the Keeper of the Privy Purse; the Director of the Royal Collection; the Comptroller of the Lord Chamberlains office dealing specifi-cally with ceremonial; the Director of Finance and Property, in charge of care and maintenance of the buildings; and the Master of the Household, a position dating back to 1539, but who, as a result of Prince Albert's reforms, is in charge of the domestic and staff arrangements as well as catering and official entertaining.

All this complex organization is run with the precision of clock-work and maintains the high standards of traditional hospitality and faultless ceremonial which have been admired features of the English royal palaces since the Middle Ages. On great occasions, Buckingham Palace still feels very much as it did in the early years of Queen Victoria's reign, and George IV would recognize in the contents and architecture of the state rooms much of his own achievement.

THE GARDEN FRONT of Buckingham
Palace in profile, showing the excellent
quality of Nash's detailing and
Croggan's coade stone decoration.